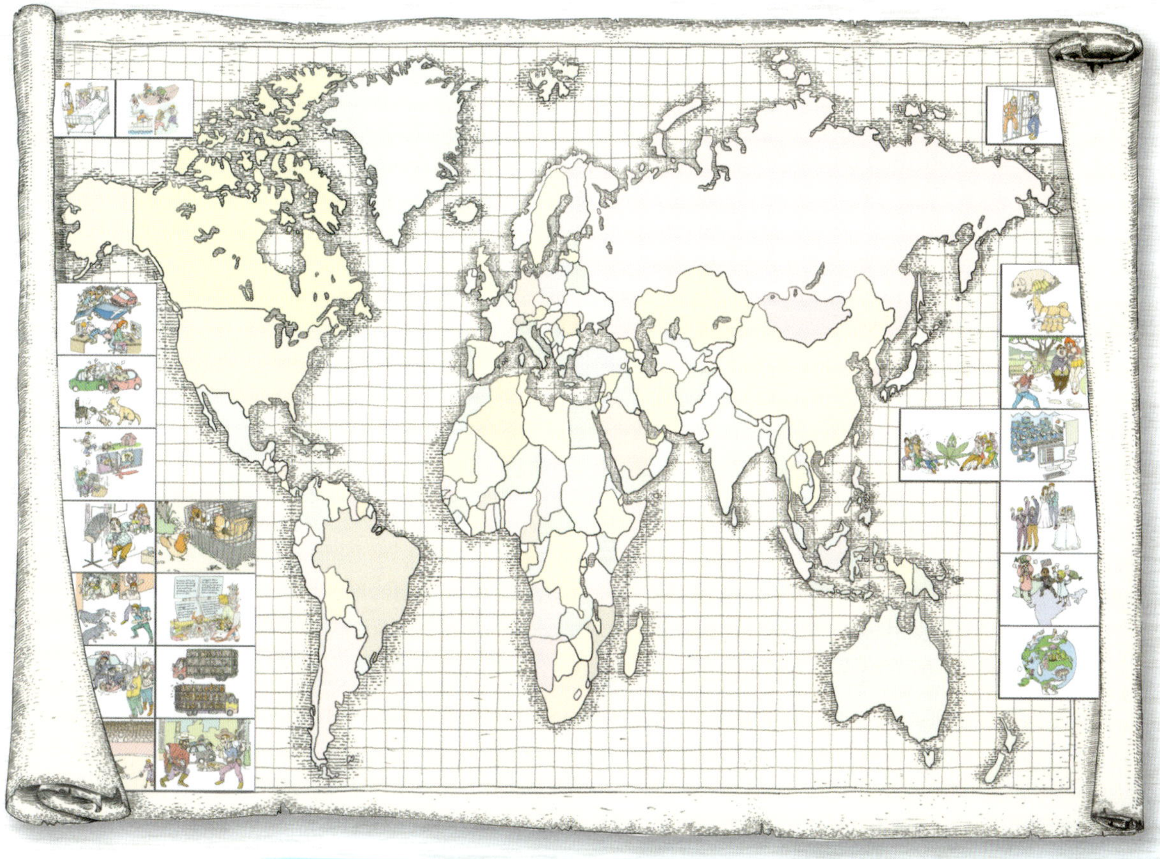

70 INTERNATIONAL ISSUES OPEN TO DEBATE

OPEN TO DEBATE 2

Introduction

This discussion book has been written for English language students who are at an intermediate or advanced level. It is intended to be a complementary volume to an earlier book written by the same author, which was entitled simply *Open to Debate*. That book dealt exclusively with issues about Korea. The present work uses the same approach and style but deals with a wide range of contemporary international issues, including topics from the realms of ethics, politics, history, society, and environment. Some issues may seem more relevant to an individual student than others. However, all the issues deal with controversial topics about which it should be easy to develop a personal opinion. At the same time, the writer has attempted to be fair to the main points of view on the various issues.

Each unit begins with a model conversation that serves to introduce the topic of the unit. These conversations use idiomatic language, the same type of language that native speakers of English are likely to use. The introductory dialogue of the unit is followed by a reading passage consisting of about 300 words. Every attempt has been made to use the most current information, statistics, and perspectives in the reading section. Finally, there are seven discussion questions that are based on the reading. The questions are designed to elicit students' opinions about the general topic, including responses about how the topic affects them personally.

Neal D. Williams

This book is dedicated to my lovely wife and best friend, Eunkyung Won.

Suggestions to the Student

Carnegie Hall in New York City was opened in 1891 and is now one of the world's most famous concert halls. Every musician dreams of performing there at some point in their career. An old joke asks the question: "How do you get to Carnegie Hall?" The answer: "Practice, practice, practice!" Many students of the English language frequently ask their teacher a similar question: "How can I become a great English speaker?" The best answer is: "Speak, speak, speak!" Of course, you have to know some grammar and vocabulary, but once you have a reasonable knowledge of those aspects, your skill in speaking English will depend on how much time you spend actually using the language.

Studies have shown that English speakers can become fairly fluent in Spanish with about 600 hours of practice. The same is true of Spanish speakers who want to learn English. The amount of time needed is fairly low because English and Spanish are somewhat similar. However, if an English speaker wants to learn Korean, that learner will need to invest about 2,200 hours of practice, and the same is true for a Korean speaker who wants to learn English. The two languages are dramatically different in appearance, grammar, and pronunciation, so much more time is needed. If you want to become a skillful English speaker, you need to accumulate as much time as possible in actually speaking the language.

One easy way to build up time in speaking English is to enroll in an English conversation class. When you are in your class, you should speak as much as you can. It is important that you not worry about using the correct grammar; just keep speaking, and you will communicate. You will also, slowly but surely, improve your conversational skills. The people who have become fluent in English are no smarter than you. They just kept trying to use English and speaking as much as possible until they gained some level of fluency. You can do the same!

Suggestions to the Teacher

If you are an English language teacher, you are naturally interested in inspiring your students to speak English as much as possible. How can this goal be accomplished? Here are several practical suggestions. First, it important to emphasize to students that the discussion questions written in this book simply provide an opportunity to express one's opinion. There is no right or wrong answer. Language experts say that one of the most important duties of a language teacher is to reduce anxiety in the classroom. Therefore, it is crucial to convince students that everyone's opinion is valid and important.

Second, because the aim of a language course is to get students involved in speaking the language as much as possible, it is better to use pair work than group discussions. When students are in groups, they may feel intimidated by more fluent speakers, and they will feel reluctant to speak. However, if they are working in pairs, they are conversing with a partner and have no choice but to speak. As they speak more with their partner, they will gain in confidence and fluency.

Third, teachers need to emphasize to students that simply trying to speak in English will help them achieve their goal of fluency. Of course, students will often experience some stress when trying to express their opinion in another language. They may feel as though their grammar and vocabulary are inadequate and that they should speak using only grammar that is completely accurate. Good teachers will explain to students that it's necessary to feel some stress, but that's not anything to worry about. Students should just keep talking, using the vocabulary and grammar that they already know. Over time, they will improve in speaking, as well as in vocabulary and grammar.

Contents

Introduction
Suggestions to the student
Suggestions to the teacher

UNIT 01 The Five Biggest Regrets before Death ······ 10
UNIT 02 Dangerous Sports ······ 12
UNIT 03 Internet Addiction ······ 14
UNIT 04 Road Rage ······ 16
UNIT 05 Frivolous Lawsuits ······ 18

UNIT 06 Domestic Violence ······ 20
UNIT 07 Cage-Free Eggs and Animal Welfare ······ 22
UNIT 08 Wasted Food ······ 24
UNIT 09 Social Networking Services ······ 26
UNIT 10 Human Trafficking ······ 28

UNIT 11 Excessive Police Violence against Minorities ······ 30
UNIT 12 Bullfighting ······ 32
UNIT 13 Gun Violence in America ······ 34
UNIT 14 Wrongfully Imprisoned ······ 36
UNIT 15 Breastfeeding in Public ······ 38

UNIT 16 Sugar Daddies and Sugar Babies ······ 40
UNIT 17 Legalization of Marijuana? ······ 42
UNIT 18 The Blame for Internet Spam ······ 44
UNIT 19 Same-Sex Marriage ······ 46
UNIT 20 Transgender Restrooms ······ 48

UNIT 21 Asian Americans: Facing Discrimination? ······ 50
UNIT 22 Eating Live Animals ······ 52
UNIT 23 Cruelty to Animals ······ 54
UNIT 24 An Apology for Hiroshima? ······ 56
UNIT 25 Fur Coats ······ 58

UNIT 26 Discrimination against Muslims ······ 60
UNIT 27 Once a Cheater, Always a Cheater? ······ 62
UNIT 28 Finding Mr./Ms. Right ······ 64
UNIT 29 Bullying in Public Schools ······ 66
UNIT 30 The Death of Marriage? ······ 68

UNIT 31 Wealthy Pastors: Truly Serving God? ······ 70
UNIT 32 Proliferation of Drones ······ 72
UNIT 33 Future Foods ······ 74
UNIT 34 Grade Inflation ······ 76
UNIT 35 Underpaid Actresses ······ 78

UNIT 36 American Universities and Chinese Students ······ 80
UNIT 37 Cosmetics for Men? ······ 82
UNIT 38 The 40-Year-Old Virgin ······ 84
UNIT 39 Secret Lottery Winners? ······ 86
UNIT 40 Male and Female: Attitudes toward Sex ······ 88

UNIT 41 Date Rape ······ 90
UNIT 42 Sexting ······ 92
UNIT 43 Cheating Students ······ 94
UNIT 44 Nonstop Hacking ······ 96
UNIT 45 Preserving the Rain Forest ······ 98

UNIT 46 Drug Cartels ······ 100
UNIT 47 Euthanasia ······ 102
UNIT 48 Israel versus Palestine ······ 104
UNIT 49 Democrats and Republicans ······ 106
UNIT 50 Racial Equality in the U.S. ······ 108

UNIT 51 Artificial Intelligence ······ 110
UNIT 52 An Apology for Slavery? ······ 112
UNIT 53 Climate Change ······ 114
UNIT 54 The British Monarchy ······ 116
UNIT 55 Climbing Mount Everest ······ 118

UNIT 56 World Religions ······ 120
UNIT 57 Scientology ······ 122
UNIT 58 China versus the U.S. ······ 124
UNIT 59 Illegal Immigration to the U.S. ······ 126
UNIT 60 The Death Penalty ······ 128

UNIT 61 Religious Veils in Public Places ······ 130
UNIT 62 Women's Rights in Saudi Arabia ······ 132
UNIT 63 Indian Housewives: Shocking Rate of Suicide ······ 134
UNIT 64 Addiction to Prescription Drugs ······ 136
UNIT 65 Claiming the Arctic and Antarctic ······ 138

UNIT 66 India versus Pakistan ······ 140
UNIT 67 The Sunni and the Shia ······ 142
UNIT 68 Chemical Weapons ······ 144
UNIT 69 A Colony on Mars? ······ 146
UNIT 70 National Foods ······ 148

OPEN TO DEBATE 2

UNIT 01

The Five Biggest Regrets before Death

John: Min-Ji, I heard that your grandfather passed away. I'm so sorry for your loss.

Min-Ji: Thank you, John. Well, he was 88 when he died, and he went peacefully.

John: Well, that's good to know. Did you talk to him just before he passed away?

Min-Ji: Actually, I did. I visited him in the hospital the day before he died.

John: Did he have any last words or memorable advice?

Min-Ji: Yes, he did. He said that he regretted working so hard during his life and not spending more time with family and friends.

John: Well, I'm sure that his generation had to work very hard just to make ends meet.

Min-Ji: Yes, that's true, but he reminded me always to spend time with those that I love.

John: That's very touching and sound advice.

— What are your biggest regrets?
— I have six regrets, including five that average people have, such as not being true to myself and working too hard.
— Then what is your last one?
— I should have gotten some life insurance! Then when I die, you would have some money.
— Why don't you do it now?
— It's too late.
— Oh, no. It's never too late! I will contact the insurance company and help you get some life insurance!

UNIT 01   The Five Biggest Regrets before Death

What regrets do dying people most often have about their lives? Fortunately, an Australian nurse named Bronnie Ware saw the value of trying to answer this question. She spent years caring for the dying and counseling them during the final weeks of their lives. She began to record their comments about their lives and any regrets that they expressed. Common themes surfaced among the patients' comments, and Bronnie recorded the top five themes in her blog. The top five regrets that people expressed were as follows:

(1) *Not being true to yourself.* Patients regretted that they had focused too much on what others expected of them and had left their own dreams unfulfilled.

(2) *Working too hard.* By focusing too much on work, patients were sad that they had missed much of their children's youth and their partner's companionship.

(3) *The courage to express your feelings.* Many people regretted that they had buried feelings of anger and bitterness inside them instead of expressing their views and dealing with issues head-on.

(4) *Distance between old friends.* True friendships are one of the most valuable possessions of life, and many patients regretted that they had let old friends slip away.

(5) *Loss of happiness.* Many people felt as though they had wasted too much time worrying and stressing about matters that were ultimately not so important. As a result, they had lost the feeling of pure happiness.

How can one avoid having regrets? One answer is to follow the advice of Steve Jobs: "For the past 33 years, I have looked in the mirror every morning and asked myself: 'If today were the last day of my life, would I want to do what I am about to do today?' And whenever the answer has been 'No' for too many days in a row, I know I need to change something."

What do you think?

(1) Have you ever talked with an older person about their life regrets? What did they say?
(2) Do you feel now that you are really fulfilling your own life's dream? Why or why not?
(3) Do you spend as much time with your family and friends as you would like?
(4) Do you feel as though you are working too hard, not hard enough, or just the right amount?
(5) On a scale of 1 to 10, how would you rank your own level of happiness nowadays?
(6) If you could change anything in your past, what would you change?
(7) Mark Twain said, "A man who lives fully is prepared to die at any time." What did he mean?

OPEN TO DEBATE 2

UNIT 02

Dangerous Sports

Kayla: The Summer Olympics are coming soon! Are you excited Min-Seok?

Min-Seok: Yes, of course. I'm looking forward to the archery and volleyball competition.

Kayla: Yeah, I like those sports. The only sport that I don't like is boxing.

Min-Seok: Oh? Why don't you like boxing?

Kayla: I think it's just too brutal and dehumanizing. There have been over 2,000 deaths in the boxing ring since the early 1700s.

Min-Seok: Oh, wow! That's shocking. I had no idea.

Kayla: Yes, it's true. There's a list you can find on the Internet that names every boxer who died in the ring.

Min-Seok: Oh, that sounds so gruesome. I don't want to see such a list.

Kayla: Yeah, it's a morbid sport, and I think it should be banned altogether.

Min-Seok: Well, I've never thought about it that much, but maybe you're right.

Let's make the world safer!

In the sport of cycling, riders must use only tricycles to avoid falling down.

The Olympics Swimming Committee is now demanding that every swimmer wear a life jacket to avoid any possibility of drowning.

In the boxing ring, boxers need to take off their gloves so they don't suffer a concussion.

UNIT 02 Dangerous Sports

At the age of 30, the boxer Peter Nebo was so battered both physically and mentally by that brutal sport that he was committed to a mental institution for the rest of his life. His friend, Manuel Velazquez (1904-1994), was sickened by what happened to Nebo, and he became a lifelong opponent of boxing. Velazquez began to compile an exhaustive list of all deaths that had occurred in the boxing ring throughout history. Though Velazquez died in 1994, the list continues and now contains the names of over 2,000 boxers who died in the ring since the early 1700s.

No boxing death was more tragic than that of the Korean Kim Duk-Koo (1955-1982). Kim grew up poor and worked odd jobs until he got into boxing in 1976. He compiled a record of 29-4 as an amateur before he turned professional in 1978. In 1982, he was scheduled to fight the American boxer Ray Mancini in a bout that was televised live on CBS. It was only his second time to fight outside of Korea. Before the fight, Kim was quoted as saying, "Either he dies or I die." For much of the fight, the two fought evenly in a very ferocious competition. Kim tore up Mancini's left ear and puffed up his left eye. Mancini's left hand swelled up to twice its normal size. However, in the latter rounds, Mancini began to dominate. In the 14th round, Mancini hit Kim with a hard right punch. Kim hit the ropes, and then his head hit the canvas. The referee stopped the fight and declared Mancini the winner by technical knockout (TKO). Minutes later, Kim collapsed into a coma and was rushed to the hospital. He died four days later.

The results of the fight were shocking. Mancini blamed himself for Kim's death and was never the same again. Three months later, Kim's mother committed suicide. The following year, the referee of the match also committed suicide. Sadly, the entire match can still be viewed on Youtube.

What do you think?

(1) Do you think that boxing should be banned as a sport due to its brutality?
(2) Can you think of any other sports that are dangerous? Should they be prohibited?
(3) Do you ever watch boxing matches on TV? Why or why not?
(4) Have you ever watched an American football game? Do you think it is a barbaric game or just a normal competitive sport?
(5) Do you think that Youtube should remove this ghastly boxing match from its website? Why or why not?
(6) Would you want your child to learn how to box? Why or why not?
(7) What do you think is the best sport for staying in good physical condition?

UNIT 03

Internet Addiction

Yu-Ri: Caleb, I think I have a problem. I need your advice.

Caleb: What sort of problem are you talking about?

Yu-Ri: I think my little brother is addicted to computer games. He's always playing this game called "World of Warcraft."

Caleb: Oh, I've heard of that. Don't your parents try to control his playing time?

Yu-Ri: Yes, they've made a strict schedule for him, but he secretly plays the game late at night when he should be sleeping.

Caleb: Oh, my! It sounds as though he is truly addicted. He needs to enter a detoxification program.

Yu-Ri: What does that mean?

Caleb: It refers to a process by which a person overcomes a physical or psychological dependency.

Yu-Ri: I see. Well, I don't know if we even have that kind of program in Korea.

Caleb: Oh, I'm sure there are such programs. Just search online for "National Center for Youth Internet Addiction Treatment."

Yu-Ri: Well, thanks for the tip!

What's happening? The monitor is sucking me in! Is this good or bad? Maybe I can join the game for real!

A life of luxury is possible on the flying carpet called Facebook!

Online shopping is based on timing. I have replaced one hand with a mouse so that I can shop more quickly and less expensively!

UNIT 03 Internet Addiction

In 1995, when the Internet was in its infancy, a psychologist coined the phrase "Internet addiction." Actually, he meant the term as a joke. Nowadays, however, Internet addiction is not a laughing matter. In 2013, Bradford Regional Medical Center in Pennsylvania opened the first-ever hospital-based Internet addiction treatment center in order to combat this increasing problem. Patients admitted to the program must have been diagnosed with a severe Internet addiction. They spend 10 days in the hospital, undergo an extensive evaluation, and experience a program referred to as a "Digital Device Detoxification Program." During a period of 72 hours, they have no access to a smart phone, a tablet, or the Internet. Instead, they attend therapy sessions and educational seminars whose focus is keep compulsive behavior under control. Participation in the program does not come cheap. Participants must pay $14,000 by cash or check at least 14 days prior to admission.

What is Internet addiction, exactly? Kimberly Young, a psychologist and founder of the program, defines Internet addiction by its consequences. Does a person's Internet obsession interfere with the normal functions of life? She explains, "Like any other addiction, we look at whether it has jeopardized their career, whether they lie about their usage, or whether it interferes with relationships." The addiction program does not try to stop addicts from using the Internet altogether; that would be unrealistic. However, they are taught how to use the Internet in a healthy way.

The stereotypical Internet addict is a young man who is highly intelligent. However, he usually suffers from low self-esteem, and he finds social interaction extremely challenging. The majority of addicts are obsessed with online games, such as "World of Warcraft," or online pornography. They are not usually obsessed with social media sites such as Facebook. In real life, they have a poor self-image, but online they can become someone else and even find admiration for their skills in playing online games.

What do you think?

(1) Do you think a 10-day in-hospital program can cure Internet addiction?
(2) What sort of treatment is available for Internet addiction in your country?
(3) Do you know anyone who shows signs of being addicted to the Internet or other digital devices?
(4) Which do you use more in a day, your smart phone or your computer?
(5) How many hours per day do you spend being connected to digital devices? Do you ever feel addicted?
(6) Do you ever play any computer games? Which ones do you play?
(7) Could you endure 72 hours without any sort of digital device? How would you react?

OPEN TO DEBATE 2

UNIT 04

Road Rage

Sarah: Ji-Hoon, you won't believe what I saw today!

Ji-Hoon: What happened?

Sarah: I was on a bus, coming to work, and our bus sideswiped a car.

Ji-Hoon: Oh, that's terrible! Was anyone hurt?

Sarah: Fortunately, no one was injured. However, the driver of the car became enraged and tried to attack the bus driver.

Ji-Hoon: Oh my! Did he injure the bus driver?

Sarah: No, because the bus driver kept the bus doors closed. However, they were arguing through the bus driver's window.

Ji-Hoon: That's terrible!

Sarah: Then the car driver put his fist through the open window and tried to hit the bus driver.

Ji-Hoon: Didn't someone call the police?

Sarah: Yes, of course. The police came in a few minutes and questioned both drivers.

Ji-Hoon: What a harrowing ordeal!

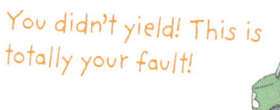
You didn't yield! This is totally your fault!

Nonsense! You must be DUI. I'm going to call the police!

It's mine! I saw it first! Go away!

No way! Let's decide by flipping a coin!

UNIT 04 Road Rage

Ken Olsen is a former police officer in Australia who has faced his share of dangerous situations while on duty. However, nothing prepared him for what happened on a December day in 2012. Without warning or provocation, a driver began ramming Olsen's car. Olsen tried to escape, but the pursuer continued, eventually hitting Olsen's car a total of seven times and running Olsen off the road. When Olsen stopped, the enraged driver jumped on the hood of Olsen's car and punched the windshield. After Olsen managed to get away, he filed charges at the local police station and revealed that he had recorded a video of the incident with his dash cam. Later, this shocking case of road rage was featured on a local Australian television show called *Today Tonight*. Olsen said, "This has shaken me. It's something that you don't expect and it's something that's very difficult to deal with. How do you deal with somebody trying to kill you on the road? I'm struggling."

After the television program broadcast aired a video clip of the incident, two other individuals came forward, stating that they also had been victims of the same raging driver. A woman told about how the driver had harassed her on the road. She said, "He is a maniac, and he should not be on the road." The third victim described a similar road rage attack by the dangerous driver a few months earlier. Police eventually charged a 21-year-old driver, Edward Sullivan, with these cases of road rage.

In Australia, road rage is considered a serious violation of law. In New South Wales, drivers who exhibit road rage can be charged with what is called "predatory driving" and sentenced for up to five years in prison, fined AUD$100,000, and disqualified from driving. However, Sullivan received a light sentence. He was disqualified from driving for six months, put on two years' probation, and ordered to pay AUD$17,000 restitution to Olsen.

What do you think?

(1) Do you think the punishment given to Sullivan was reasonable? Why or why not?
(2) What sort of punishment can drivers receive for road rage in your country?
(3) Have you ever witnessed a case of road rage? What happened?
(4) Have you ever been the victim of road rage yourself? What happened?
(5) Do you have a driver's license? How old were you when you received it? How often do you drive?
(6) If you are driving, and another driver shows anger toward you, how do you respond?
(7) Do know anyone who owns a dash cam? Do they use it every day?

OPEN TO DEBATE 2

UNIT 05

Frivolous Lawsuits

Isabella: Dong-Woo, do you know any lawyers?

Dong-Woo: Yes, I do. My uncle is a lawyer. Why? Are you in some kind of trouble?

Isabella: No, not at all. I'm just thinking about suing someone.

Dong-Woo: Really? Who do you want to sue?

Isabella: The director of the institute where I teach English. I think he's not paying me according to my contract.

Dong-Woo: I see. Well, I think there's a way that you can avoid going to court.

Isabella: Really? What can I do?

Dong-Woo: Check out the website of the Korea Ministry of Employment and Labor. They enforce the labor laws in Korea.

Isabella: Hmmm... That sounds like a good idea. I'll do that.

Dong-Woo: You should. It's their job to help anyone who is experiencing unfair labor practices.

Isabella: Sounds good. Thanks for the tip!

This dog is scaring me to death! I'm going to sue the owner!

This guy's noise is driving me crazy! I'm going to sue him!

What? Another blackout? I was in the middle of my video game! I'm going to sue the power company!

Don't these problems seem frivolous? Not to these people! What seems trivial to one person is a life-and-death matter to another.

UNIT 05 Frivolous Lawsuits

In 2005, a lawsuit was filed in Washington, DC, that shocked the world. An administrative law judge named Roy L. Pearson, Jr., filed suit against Soo Chung, Jin Nam Chung, and Ki Y. Chung, three Korean owners of a dry cleaning business called Custom Cleaners. The dry cleaners displayed a sign that read "satisfaction guaranteed," and Mr. Pearson was not satisfied because the dry cleaners did not have his trousers cleaned and ready by a certain date. When the dry cleaners found the pants a few days later, Pearson refused to accept them. He demanded a payment of more than $1,000, which the dry cleaners refused. In response, Pearson filed a lawsuit, which became known as "Pearson v. Chung," or simply the "pants lawsuit." Pearson demanded $67 million as compensation for the inconvenience, mental anguish, and attorney's fees, although he represented himself. Later, he reduced his demands to $54 million. On June 25, 2007, the trial ended when the judge overseeing the trial ruled in favor of the dry cleaners. In spite of that decision, Pearson continued to appeal his case, which finally ended on March 2, 2009, when the Court of Appeals rejected Pearson's request for reconsideration. Meanwhile, the Chungs faced legal bills of $100,000, but these fees were eventually covered by donations.

Largely because of this ridiculous lawsuit, Pearson's tenure as a judge was not renewed, and he had to enter private practice. However, that was not the end. On June 3, 2016, the Washington DC Board on Professional Responsibility ruled that Pearson had committed two ethics violations by presenting arguments that were not supported by facts or law and by interfering with the administration of justice. The Board recommended that Pearson be put on probation for two years as a practicing lawyer. The Board did not explain why they took over 10 years to recommend professional discipline for Pearson.

Legal experts cite this case as indisputable evidence that the American legal system is in need of serious reform.

What do you think?

(1) Have you heard of any other frivolous lawsuits? What happened?
(2) How does your country's legal system handle frivolous or vexatious lawsuits?
(3) Have you or someone you know ever filed a lawsuit? What was the basis of the lawsuit?
(4) Many Americans have a very low opinion of lawyers. Is that attitude prevalent in your country?
(5) Lawyers in the U.S. can even advertise to try and get new clients. Is that possible in your country?
(6) Is it expensive to hire a lawyer in your country? What is the usual rate per hour?
(7) Do you trust the legal system in your country to make the right decisions in most cases?

OPEN TO DEBATE 2

UNIT 06

Domestic Violence

Jacob: Da-Eun, how are you doing today?

Da-Eun: I'm not doing so well, I'm afraid.

Jacob: Oh? What's wrong?

Da-Eun: My friend's mom is being abused by her husband.

Jacob: Oh, that's terrible! Is it physical or emotional abuse?

Da-Eun: Both. He gets drunk sometimes, and that's when he yells at her and even strikes her.

Jacob: That's just awful! Why doesn't she report him to the police?

Da-Eun: Well, she did once, but the police just talked to the man and tried to calm him down. They didn't do anything else.

Jacob: That's a shame. I think that she should try to get out of that house.

Da-Eun: Yeah, I agree, but she always says that she wants "to keep the family together."

Jacob: Well, that's a noble goal, up to a point, but if you're physically abused, you need to leave.

Da-Eun: I agree wholeheartedly. I hope she leaves soon.

Don't move and be quiet. He's drunk now, but maybe he'll be okay tomorrow.

I'm scared. We'd better call the police!

No way! It will make him even angrier, and he'll hit us instead of the punching bag.

I'm not a violent man by nature. I don't hit anyone unless they deserve it!

UNIT 06 Domestic Violence

Domestic violence goes by many terms: intimate partner violence, battering, relationship abuse, spousal abuse, or family violence. Whatever term is used, the intent is to refer to a pattern of behavior where one person establishes control over another through fear and intimidation or through the use of actual violence. Domestic violence can happen to anyone, regardless of income, social status, gender, ethnicity, or other factors. While we usually treat domestic violence as a crime against women, it is also an offense that can be directed at men as well.

The World Health Organization classifies domestic violence as a major public health problem and a violation of human rights. According to the WHO research released in early 2016, approximately 35% of women worldwide have experienced either physical and/or sexual violence. While this sort of violence can come from a non-partner, most of the violence is from an intimate partner. Indeed, 30% of women who have been involved in a relationship with a man report that they have been the victims of some form of physical and/or sexual violence committed by their intimate partner. In fact, as many as 38% of the murders committed against women around the world are committed by an intimate partner.

Studies of domestic violence in the United States show that it is most likely to take place between 6 pm and 6 am. Also, more than 60% of domestic violence incidents happen at home. Domestic violence is the third leading cause of homelessness among families. At least one-third of the families using New York City's family shelter system are homeless because of domestic violence. The group that is at the greatest risk of domestic violence consists of women who are aged 18 to 34. More than three million American children witness domestic violence every year, and children who live in homes where domestic violence takes place often suffer abuse and neglect at very high rates.

What do you think?

(1) Are you shocked by the statistics cited by the World Health Organization? What is the most shocking?
(2) Is domestic violence a serious problem in your country?
(3) Do you personally know someone who has been a victim of domestic violence? What happened?
(4) Do you know of any cases where a man has been the victim of domestic violence? What happened?
(5) What sort of punishment should a man get if he hits his wife? Should he go to jail?
(6) If your relative or close friend were a victim of domestic violence, what advice would you offer?
(7) What steps can we take to reduce the incidence of domestic violence?

UNIT 07

Cage-Free Eggs and Animal Welfare

Ethan: Hye-Jin, do you know if McDonald's in Korea uses cage-free eggs?

Hye-Jin: What does "cage-free" mean? I'm not familiar with that term.

Ethan: It means that the eggs are laid by hens that have a freedom of movement. They are not housed in tiny cages.

Hye-Jin: I see. Well, I've never seen that kind of label on eggs sold in Korea.

Ethan: In Canada, where I'm from, less than 10% of eggs are cage-free, but you can usually find them in large supermarkets.

Hye-Jin: Maybe you can find them in a specialty store here, like an organic food store.

Ethan: Do you know where I could find such a store?

Hye-Jin: I know of one in Apgujeong. I can take you there sometime, if you like.

Ethan: Oh, that sounds great. How about this coming Saturday?

Hye-Jin: Okay, I'm free then. We can do it.

Don't even think about it! If you fail, you'll be put to death immediately!

— Why are you inside that cage?
— We've been kept here since we were little to produce eggs.
— That's terrible! How can you keep laying eggs there? It's like you're in jail!
— That's so true! We're miserable.
— Why don't you escape?
— How can we?
— I'll bring you a DVD entitled *The Shawshank Redemption*. I'm sure it'll help you.

UNIT 07 — Cage-Free Eggs and Animal Welfare

Grocery shoppers in Canada and the United States are often puzzled when they come to the egg display in their local supermarket. They are confronted with an array of egg cartons labeled "free run," "free range," "organic," or "cage-free." Unfortunately, there is no fixed definition of these terms, but many consumers are now starting to choose eggs that come from hens that are given a free range of movement. More and more, the term that is being used for such eggs is "cage-free." At present, more than 90% of eggs in Canada and the U.S. come from chickens that spend their entire lives in what are called "battery cages." These cages can house up to 12 chickens, which gives each bird about 67 square inches (432 square centimeters) of space, which is about the size of an iPad. Because of such restricted space, the hens cannot engage in their fundamental biological needs, such as foraging, wing-flapping, perching, and nesting.

Commercial egg producers claim that this traditional method of egg production within cages is safe and that it keeps egg prices low. However, more and more consumers are demanding that eggs be produced in cage-free housing, where hens can stretch their wings and move about freely in an open barn. Large companies have taken notice of the campaign for cage-free eggs and are making plans to switch to cage-free eggs. In 2015, McDonald's announced that it would slowly phase in the use of cage-free eggs, but it would take a 10-year period to complete the transition. Subway, the world's largest fast-food chain, announced that it will end the use of eggs laid by caged hens in its U.S. locations by the year 2025. The policy is already in effect in Subway's European and Australian locations. Nestlé, the world's biggest food producer, pledged to make a complete transition to cage-free eggs within five years. Starbucks claimed that its egg supply would be cage-free by 2020.

What do you think?

(1) Are you familiar with cage-free eggs? Is this product available in your country?
(2) Do you agree with advocates of animal welfare that raising hens in battery cages is cruel and inhumane?
(3) Would you be willing to pay slightly higher prices for cage-free eggs?
(4) Why do you think it is taking companies so many years to change to cage-free eggs?
(5) Can you think of any other practices of raising animals for food that could be classified as inhumane?
(6) In some countries, sows (female pigs) are kept in narrow spaces or even chained to the floor. Is this a cruel practice? Is it allowed in your country?
(7) Brad Pitt criticized Costco until it agreed to switch to cage-free eggs. Should actors be admired for such activism for animal welfare?

UNIT 08

Wasted Food

Tony: Hyun-Ji, I have a question about Korean culture.

Hyun-Ji: Okay. What's your question?

Tony: When I eat a meal at a Korean restaurant, there are always a lot of side dishes.

Hyun-Ji: Yeah, that's an essential part of Korean food culture.

Tony: Yeah, but often my friends and I cannot finish all the side dishes. What happens to that extra food?

Hyun-Ji: In most cases, it's just thrown away, or it goes into a food waste bin, and it's eventually eaten by pigs.

Tony: Do restaurants ever re-use uneaten food on side dishes?

Hyun-Ji: I think that most restaurants do not, but there might be some very cheap restaurants that re-use uneaten side dishes.

Tony: Re-serving side dishes seems gross, but wasting all that food is troublesome too.

Hyun-Ji: I agree with you. Restaurants need to serve smaller portions of side dishes that people can finish eating.

Tony: Yeah, they could do that. Also, they could charge a little extra if people don't finish their all their food.

Hyun-Ji: Hmmm... I'm not sure that would work.

— This is our block. Go away!
— What do you mean "your block"? All that food has been thrown away. We have a right to eat it if we want!
— Can't you see the sign? Dogs are not allowed here!
— That's ridiculous! That sign means "dogs are welcome!"

UNIT 08 Wasted Food

In early 2016, France became the first country in the world to prohibit supermarkets from throwing away or destroying unsold food that is still edible. Instead of throwing away the food, the supermarkets are being forced to donate the food to charitable organizations and food banks for the poor. In addition, supermarkets will be barred from intentionally spoiling food in an effort to thwart people from foraging in the stores' garbage bins. In recent years, many families, students, and homeless people have begun to search through supermarket bins and dumpsters at night in order to find food. In many cases, supermarkets throw out food because it has nearly reached its "best before" date, but the food is still edible. France has been wasting seven million tons of food annually. Carrefour, a huge supermarket chain in France, welcomed the law, agreeing that it would help increase food donations. Charitable organizations also welcomed the news because the new policy will enable them to give out millions more free meals to people who often struggle to find the money just to eat.

The new law was largely in response to a grassroots campaign conducted by French shoppers, anti-poverty campaigners, and citizens opposed to food waste. Supporters of the law hope that the rest of the European Union will adopt similar provisions. The new law will apply to supermarkets that have 400 square meters or more of space. The stores will have to sign donation contracts with charitable entities or face a fine of 3,750 Euros. Jacques Bailet, head of Banques Alimentaires, an association of French food banks, responded to the law positively, saying, "Because supermarkets will be obliged to sign a donation deal with charities, we'll be able to increase the quality and diversity of food we get and distribute. In terms of nutritional balance, we currently have a deficit of meat and a lack of fruit and vegetables. This will hopefully allow us to push for those products."

What do you think?

(1) Is food waste a problem in your country? What types of food are wasted?
(2) Do you think a law similar to the French one should be passed in your country? Why or why not?
(3) What organizations exist in your country to help provide food to poor people?
(4) Have you ever donated money to help the poor and disadvantaged? Where did you make your donation?
(5) Have you ever thrown away edible food? Why did you throw it away?
(6) Did your parents ever tell you, "Clean your plate; many people are starving"? Did you clean your plate? Do you still clean your plate today?
(7) Some religious people say that wasting food is a sin. Do you agree with that idea?

OPEN TO DEBATE 2

UNIT 09

Social Networking Services

Ji-Seong: Alyssa, do you have a Facebook® account?

Alyssa: I do actually. Why do you ask?

Ji-Seong: Could I be your Facebook friend?

Alyssa: Yes, of course, but I must tell you that I rarely use my Facebook account.

Ji-Seong: Oh? Why not?

Alyssa: Frankly speaking, I find it to be a waste of time. I only use it occasionally for posting pictures that my family can see.

Ji-Seong: Okay. No problem. Have you ever unfriended anyone?

Alyssa: Yes, I have two times.

Ji-Seong: May I ask why you unfriended them?

Alyssa: Well, a couple of Facebook friends kept posting risqué photos that I thought were very inappropriate.

Ji-Seong: I see. Well, I don't do that sort of thing, so I don't think you'll ever need to unfriend me.

— I'm always so busy doing SNS, including Facebook, Instagram, Tumblr, and Twitter! So I have no time to look for a job, to meet friends, or to feed my baby. But I'm so happy because I have a lot of "real" friends online. I'm absolutely sure they will do everything for me when I'm in trouble.
— Daddy! What're you doing? I'm starving!
— Be quiet! Don't you see I'm busy? Aren't you old enough to feed yourself?

UNIT 09 Social Networking Services

A social networking service (SNS), a form of social media, is a platform that is used to build social relations among people who share similar interests. When utilizing an SNS, users provide their own individual profiles and content. Popular SNS platforms in the United States include Facebook, Google+, LinkedIn, Instagram, Tumblr, and Twitter. Other countries have localized platforms, such as Weibo in China and Nexopia in Canada. In 2016, 78% of Americans had a social network profile.

The advantages of social media are numerous. For one thing, social networking obviously creates new social connections for individuals. Users can keep in touch with family and friends, but they can also make new friends. In addition, some students do better in school because they can use such sites to discuss schoolwork and educational topics. Another major benefit of an SNS lies in the level of support that one can find. Support groups where people can discuss health needs, including emotional issues, are everywhere. Social media can also serve as a source of employment. Statistics show that 89% of job recruiters have used sites such as LinkedIn. Finally, social media are being used by police departments to nab criminals who are foolish enough to brag online about their criminal activities.

Social media also possess some drawbacks. The most noticeable one is that such sites are used by sexual predators to find victims. Also, many SNS platforms are nothing more than rumor mills that spread misinformation about health, education, politics, celebrities, and non-celebrities. Another disadvantage of social media is that some students are tempted to spend too much time on such sites, resulting in lower grades than students who don't use an SNS at all. The use of social media is also frequently blamed for loss of productivity in the workplace. Finally, one obvious criticism that can be leveled against social media is that it is a direct cause for less face-to-face communication. One study showed that 32% of people admitted using texting or an SNS during family gatherings.

What do you think?

(1) Can you think of other advantages and disadvantages not mentioned in the reading passage?
(2) How many types of social media do you use? Do you use any of them every day?
(3) Have you read any stories about criminals being caught because of their social media posts?
(4) Would you allow your children to have private social media accounts that you can never see?
(5) Have you tried finding an old friend on social media? What happened?
(6) Have you made any new friends in other countries through social media? Where do they live?
(7) Do you think it is rude to send text messages or access SNS when meeting family or friends?

OPEN TO DEBATE 2

UNIT 10

Human Trafficking

Joseph: Ji-Hye, did you read the stories about the forced labor on the salt evaporation farms in Sinan County in Jeollanam-do?

Ji-Hye: Yes, I did. It's shocking and a shameful event in modern Korean history.

Joseph: Well, human trafficking takes place in some form in every country in the world.

Ji-Hye: Of course, that's true, but what happened in Sinan Country was just awful.

Joseph: Yeah, I read that two disabled men were forced to work 14 hours per day without pay.

Ji-Hye: That's true, and they were beaten if they didn't work hard enough.

Joseph: How were they freed from this terrible situation?

Ji-Hye: One of the men managed to write his mother, and then she contacted the police.

Joseph: Well, at least they have been freed now.

Ji-Hye: Yes, and the police investigated every single salt evaporation farm and freed all forced laborers.

Joseph: Well, that's good to hear.

Ji-Hye: Absolutely! This should never happen in the 21st century.

Only a small percentage of humans are victims of human trafficking while all pigs are victims of animal trafficking. It's time that humans solved the problems of animal trafficking before they tackle their own trafficking problems.

Are you kidding? It's your destiny to end up like this!

At least we should be treated and carried with decency before being slaughtered. We want to be carried in a LIMOUSINE! Is it too much to ask as our last wish?

Treated with decency? You must be kidding! You're going to be put to death in a moment!

UNIT 10 Human Trafficking

Moldova has a population of less than 3,000,000 people, but it has become a shocking source of human trafficking, with as many as 25,000 Moldovans falling prey to trafficking gangs each year. About 10% of the victims are children. According to an article in the British newspaper *Daily Mail*, one such victim was Irina. Her home life was incredibly tragic. Her mother died of breast cancer, and she was raped by her own father. He was sent to prison for that terrible crime, leaving her in the care of her godmother, who suggested that she go to Turkey saying, "The conditions are much better there, and they'll look after you."

When Irina arrived at the airport in Istanbul, she was met by two men who drove her to a property where there were three other girls. She was instructed to "serve" their clients. There was no chance to escape, and she had no choice but to serve twelve or more men per day. Her captors took all the money she earned, telling her that she owed for air flights and accommodation. Her bruises and cuts were covered up with cheap cosmetics. After a few weeks, she managed to use the cell phone of one of her clients and call a friend that she knew in Dubai. Her friend helped her to escape by reporting her situation to a charity organization that enabled her to return to Moldova.

Irina is one of 20.9 million victims of human trafficking, which is a $150 billion industry worldwide, according to experts. About 68% of these victims are trapped in forced labor, 26% of them are children, and 55% are women and girls. The U.S. Department of Labor has identified 136 products from 74 countries made by forced labor and child labor. Researchers conclude that human trafficking is the "slavery of the modern age," and it affects every country in the world.

What do you think?

(1) Does human trafficking take place in your country? What forms does it take?
(2) Does your government have any counter-trafficking laws? Are they strictly enforced?
(3) What sort of punishment should be faced by criminals engaged in human trafficking?
(4) Do you support any human rights organizations, such as Amnesty International or Human Rights Watch?
(5) Have you ever watched a film or documentary about human trafficking? What was your response?
(6) Would you visit a country as a tourist if you knew it tolerated human trafficking?
(7) Would you buy a product if you knew it was produced using child labor?

OPEN TO DEBATE 2

UNIT 11

Excessive Police Violence against Minorities

Jack: Yu-Na, I have a question for you.

Yu-Na: Sure. What's your question?

Jack: Do you have any black friends?

Yu-Na: Hmmm… Actually, I don't know any black people at all. There just aren't many black people living in Korea.

Jack: So you've never met a black person?

Yu-Na: Oh, I've met a couple of black students before. One of my friends at another university introduced us. However, I just saw them that one time.

Jack: I see. Well, do you think that black people face discrimination in Korea?

Yu-Na: I don't think so, actually. Certainly, most young Koreans are accepting of people from all races.

Jack: How would Koreans feel if their son or daughter wanted to marry a black person?

Yu-Na: Some older conservative people might object, but I think that most Koreans would approve.

Jack: Well, that's good to hear.

Don't complain! We ALWAYS treat black and white people equally. We're just LESS interested in white people's crimes.

Why are you abusing me? What did I do wrong? Why don't you arrest those two white gang members standing there?

Hooray! This is real democracy!

UNIT 11
Excessive Police Violence against Minorities

On February 8, 2015, Natasha McKenna, a young African-American woman, was in police custody in Fairfax County, Virginia, in the United States. She suffered from psychological disorders, having been diagnosed with schizophrenia, bi-polar disorder, and depression. When police came to transport her to another location, she resisted their efforts. In response, the police used a Taser type of stun gun on her 17 times. After being Tasered, McKenna suffered cardiac arrest, lost consciousness, and eventually died from her injuries. No police officers were charged with a crime for the death of Natasha McKenna.

Sadly, the death of this African-American woman is representative of a continuing crisis faced by African-American citizens: the fact that they are killed by police at an excessive rate. In the U.S., black people represent approximately 13% of the population, but the rate at which they are killed by police is more than twice the rate of white people. Statistics from 2015 show that Americans were killed by police at the following rates per million: blacks, 7.13; Hispanics, 3.48; Native Americans, 3.4; whites, 2.91; Asians, 1.34. Nearly 1/3 of black people killed by police in 2015 were actually unarmed. Out of the 102 cases in 2015 where an unarmed black person was killed by police, only 10 cases resulted in any officers being charged with a crime. Out of those 10 cases, only two officers were convicted.

In response to these shocking statistics, the African-American community formed a movement called "Black Lives Matter." The group organizes protests around the deaths of black people who are killed by police officers, as well as campaigning for improvements in the broader issues of racial inequality in the U.S. criminal justice system.

What do you think?

(1) Are you familiar with the Black Lives Matter movement? What is your opinion of it?
(2) Who are the main minorities in your country? What percentage are they of the overall population?
(3) Do you think that minorities in your country face any sort of discrimination?
(4) Does your country have strict laws that punish crimes against minorities?
(5) Do you have any friends or acquaintances that are from a minority? Are they from an ethnic or religious minority?
(6) Universities are accepting increasing numbers of international students and professors. Do you think they are treated well in your country?
(7) Would you consider dating someone from a minority group? How about marrying a minority person?

OPEN TO DEBATE 2

UNIT 12

Bullfighting

Randy: Hi So-Yeon. Do you have any plans for the weekend?

So-Yeon: Actually, I do. I'm going down to Cheongdo with a friend. We're going to watch a bullfight.

Randy: What? A bullfight in Korea?

So-Yeon: Sure! Cheongdo has held a bullfighting festival since 1999. They even have a huge stadium for the event.

Randy: Wow! I had no idea. Do they have matadors, like in Spain?

So-Yeon: No, there are no matadors, and the bulls do not die. They only butt heads until one bull yields.

Randy: I see. So it's a kind of bloodless bullfighting.

So-Yeon: Yeah, and because of that, it's not so controversial.

Be thankful you had a chance to participate in the greatest sport in the world! Sorry but it's time for me to take your life! Do you have any last words?

You have a sword, and I don't! How can that be fair? Why not give me a sword too? You are just a coward in a fancy costume! This is not a sport. It's just a SLAUGHTER!

UNIT 12 Bullfighting

Bullfighting is a traditional sport of Spain, Portugal, some parts of France, and several Latin American countries. It is often referred to as an example of a "blood sport," which is a sport or type of entertainment that involves the shedding of blood. However, in the countries where bullfighting takes place, people do not classify it as a sport but regard it as a cultural event and a form of art. The main aspect of bullfighting occurs when professional bullfighters, or *toreros*, make various formal motions toward the bull, and many of these motions conclude by hooking the bull with a sword behind the shoulder. Finally, the bull is killed by the most senior bullfighter, who is called a *matador*. Of course, there is tremendous danger faced by the bullfighters, and during the past three centuries, more than 500 bullfighters have died in the ring or from injuries received from a bull.

In the modern world, bullfighting has become a very controversial sport because of its effect on the animal. Advocates of animal welfare regard bullfighting as a cruel and barbaric sport because it causes severe stress for the bull and usually leads to a slow and agonizing death. Indeed, the trend seems to be against bullfighting because it is now banned in numerous countries, including some Latin American areas where it used to be popular. Some countries allow a form of bloodless bullfighting of person against bull or bull against bull. On the other hand, proponents of bullfighting regard it as a deeply ingrained part of their local culture. Supporters argue that a bull raised for bullfighting actually lives 4-6 years and is treated very well during its lifetime. Its life is longer than that of a cow raised for meat, whose lifetime is only 1-2 years, and who may suffer more when slaughtered for food than a bull does at the end of a bullfight.

What do you think?

(1) Is bullfighting a cruel sport that should be banned?
(2) Do you agree with traditionalists that bullfighting is an art form, not a sport?
(3) Does your country permit bullfighting? What about bloodless bullfighting?
(4) Do countries have a right to criticize other countries' cultural practices?
(5) If you visited Spain, would you attend a bullfight as a cultural event?
(6) Can you think of any other sports that might involve animal cruelty (e.g., cockfighting)?
(7) What is your opinion of human-against-human sports that involve violence (e.g., boxing)?

UNIT 13

Gun Violence in America

Ji-Nah: Alex, you are from America, right?

Alex: Yes, I'm from Virginia, which is a southern state.

Ji-Nah: May I ask you a personal question?

Alex: Sure, if it's not too personal. Go ahead.

Ji-Nah: Many Americans own guns. How about you? Do you own a gun?

Alex: Well, I used to. When I was growing up, I lived in an area where hunting was popular.

Ji-Nah: I see. So you used to go hunting?

Alex: Yes, when I was young, I did. However, after I went to college, I was too busy with my studies, and I never went hunting again.

Ji-Nah: What happened to your gun?

Alex: I sold it for about $200, and I never bought another one. I have no interest now in owning a gun, and I wish that it was more difficult for people to buy a gun.

Ji-Nah: Well, I'm happy to hear that.

A gunfight in broad daylight! Where are the police?

We're scared too. Now that everybody has the freedom to bear arms, people need to take care of themselves and protect themselves with guns. We are powerless in these circumstances.

— This is a fair way to settle our differences, isn't it?
— I agree. But we used to be best friends. It's too bad that one of us has to die. Isn't there another way we could settle our disagreement?
— You make a good point. Why don't we just flip a coin?

UNIT 13 — Gun Violence in America

The year 2015 was another year of shocking gun violence in the United States. In Houston, Texas, a man shot to death his ex-girlfriend, her husband, and six children. In Charleston, South Carolina, at the oldest black church in the southern U.S., a crazed white youth joined a Bible study but then pulled out a gun and killed nine African-American worshippers. In Moneta, Virginia, two young reporters were shot to death during a live news broadcast. The shocking number of incidents in 2015 only increased in 2016. According to the website gunviolencearchive.org, there were 53,270 incidents involving gun violence in the U.S. during 2015. Among these, 13,429 people were killed (about 37 per day), and 27,001 were injured. A total of 698 children, aged 0-11, were killed or injured, and among children aged 12-17, there were 2,693 killed or injured. Also, there were 1,965 incidents of accidental shootings that ended in death or injury.

Gun violence is so prevalent in the United States that many people who live outside the U.S. frequently ask, "Why does the world's most powerful democratic nation continue to endure such extreme gun violence?" In response, the first observation that one can make is that, according to experts, the percentage of American households with a gun has been steadily declining, from 54% in 1977 to 33% in 2009. However, at the same time, the average number of guns per owner has increased from 4.1 in 1994 to 6.9 in 2004. Also, the percentage of Americans who die from gun violence has actually been decreasing. In 1993, the rate of homicides was 7.0 for every 100,000 people; in 2013, the percentage had fallen to 3.6. However, the U.S. remains a very violent country. The second observation to make about gun issues in the U.S. is that the second amendment to the constitution allows citizens to own guns. There is a significant proportion of American society that fiercely opposes any attempts to limit the freedom to buy guns. Any measures introduced in Congress to restrict gun ownership are usually defeated or severely watered down in their effects. It seems that this issue will not be solved by the current generation.

What do you think?

(1) What steps should the U.S. take in order to reduce gun violence?
(2) If you planned a visit to the U.S., would you be worried about gun violence?
(3) In your country, how easy is it to buy a gun? Can anyone buy a gun?
(4) In some countries, such as Korea and Japan, the rate of gun violence is very low. Why is that true?
(5) Are there legitimate reasons for owning a gun? Would you like to own one?
(6) Have you ever fired a gun? Would you like to visit a shooting range and practice firing?
(7) If you found out that your best friend owned a gun, how would you react?

OPEN TO DEBATE 2

UNIT 14

Wrongfully Imprisoned

Nicholas: Ji-Yeon, I'm curious about something. Does Korea have the death penalty?

Ji-Yeon: Yeah, it's a law on the books. However, no one has actually been executed for a long time.

Nicholas: Hmmm... that's interesting. When was the last time that someone was actually put to death?

Ji-Yeon: I think it was back in 1997. However, there are about 60 people on death row in Korea right now.

Nicholas: Do you think they will eventually be executed?

Ji-Yeon: I doubt it. There seems to be a trend against the death penalty in our modern society.

Nicholas: I see. Well, personally I think that's a good trend. I cannot support capital punishment.

Ji-Yeon: I can understand your opposition, but I haven't fully made up my mind on this issue just yet.

— You know that I'm innocent! Let me out right now! I want a retrial!
— I know you're innocent. But a retrial is impossible until the real criminal is arrested.
— Then what will happen if the real killer is not caught?
— You will serve life in prison.
— You know I'm innocent of the crime, and you put me in prison wrongfully! Why?
— Justice must be served under any circumstances. But if the real killer is caught, you'll be set free, and you'll get a lot of money. You'll be a millionaire!
— Yeah, but it's more likely that I'll stay here for a lifetime with no compensation!
— True, but haven't you heard the old saying "No risk, no result"?

UNIT 14 — Wrongfully Imprisoned

In 1984, a terrible crime happened in North Carolina. Deborah Sykes, a 25-year-old newspaper editor, was stabbed to death on her way to work. Eventually, Darryl Hunt was arrested and convicted of the murder. He was sentenced to life in prison, though he always maintained his innocence. In addition, the case was tainted with racial overtones: the victim was a white woman, and the accused was a black man. Some people thought that there had been a rush to judgment, and perhaps Hunt might be innocent. Others believed that the right man had been convicted, and justice had been served. Hunt languished in prison for more than 19 years before he was proven innocent based on DNA testing as well as a confession by the actual criminal, Willard E. Brown. Darryl Hunt, released from prison, became eligible to receive $20,000 for each year that he was wrongly imprisoned.

Darryl Hunt is just one of 337 people whose guilty verdicts have been overturned through the work of the Innocence Project. Among that group, there were 20 prisoners who were actually on death row, waiting to be executed. The Innocence Project was established in 1992 to determine if prisoners had been falsely convicted. In fact, studies have shown that incorrect identification by eyewitnesses of crimes had been a factor in over 70% of wrongful convictions. The Innocence Project has used DNA evidence to exonerate many prisoners of the crimes for which they were convicted. The fact that some of those freed prisoners were nearly executed for crimes that they did not commit has fueled increasing opposition to the death penalty in the United States. Some experts claim that 4% of persons sentenced to death during recent decades were probably innocent.

In spite of the victories by the Innocence Project, some judges continue to challenge these exonerations based on DNA evidence. U.S. Supreme Court Chief Justice John Roberts said that such DNA testing runs the risk of "overthrowing the established system of criminal justice."

What do you think?

(1) Do you think $20,000 for each year of false imprisonment is adequate compensation for Mr. Hunt?
(2) Is there an organization like the Innocence Project in your country?
(3) Have you read about similar exonerations of prisoners in your country?
(4) Do you believe that the death penalty is an effective deterrent for criminals?
(5) Have you ever witnessed a crime in progress? What happened?
(6) If you saw a crime occur, would you help the police and testify in court?
(7) Someone has said, "It's better that ten guilty persons go free than one innocent person be convicted." Do you agree with this idea?

OPEN TO DEBATE 2

UNIT 15

Breast Feeding in Public

Chloe: Joon-Ho, I've lived in Korea now for five years, and there's something that I've never seen.

Joon-Ho: What's that?

Chloe: A woman breastfeeding a baby in public.

Joon-Ho: Oh, I'm not surprised. Korean mothers don't usually breastfeed in public.

Chloe: Well, in Canada, where I'm from, you can easily see a nursing mother anywhere in public.

Joon-Ho: Korean women are very modest, and they just don't do that.

Chloe: What do they do?

Joon-Ho: They go to a private room or, if they do breastfeed in public, they use some type of cover.

Chloe: I see. Well, when babies get a few months old, they tend to push covers away, so they can see what's going on around them.

Joon-Ho: In that case, I think that a Korean woman would go to a private area.

Chloe: Well, it's a shame that Korean society is not more open to such a natural activity.

Joon-Ho: I see your point.

Human females are not allowed to breast-feed their babies in public places. It's unnatural! They're living under a dictatorship!

I don't think so. It has nothing to do with the political system. They just need to seize their maternal rights.

I'm so lucky that I was born a pig. I can suck mom's nipple whenever I'm hungry!

I wish I could be a human baby, even if I'd go hungry.

UNIT 15 Breast Feeding in Public

Should a woman be allowed to breastfeed in public? Answers to that question vary across the world. In 2009, a woman named Tanya Constable entered her local Walmart store in Langford, British Columbia, Canada. She was accompanied by her 11-month-old daughter, Myra, who began to cry. Ms. Constable immediately began to breastfeed the child but was approached by a store employee who told her that she couldn't breastfeed in public. Instead, she should go to the ladies' room. She refused and asked to speak to a manager, but the manager supported the employee's directive. Then Ms. Constable left the store. When the story became public, Walmart Canada apologized for the entire episode, admitting that it was wrong for the employee to tell the customer to move to the ladies' room. In fact, Walmart Canada stated that the official policy of the store is that nursing mothers can breastfeed in whatever manner they choose anywhere in the store.

Similar situations have been faced by nursing mothers in the United States. In 2011, Michelle Hickman was breastfeeding her baby at the back of a Target store in Houston, Texas. Even though her baby was covered, she was asked by two employees to move to a fitting room. One employee even remarked, "You can be reported for indecent exposure." Ms. Hickman told about this harassment on her Facebook page, and in response, nursing mothers across the U.S. organized public "nurse-ins" at Target stores in various American cities. During a "nurse-in," many mothers come in as a group and breastfeed their babies together. In response, Target established very clear policies about breastfeeding, which all employees were required to know. The full policy is stated as follows: "Guests may openly breastfeed in our stores."

What do you think?

(1) Have you heard about any breastfeeding controversies like the ones described above?
(2) Do you think that nursing mothers should be able to breastfeed anywhere in public?
(3) Have you ever seen a mother breastfeed in a public place? Did she use a cover?
(4) In your opinion, for how many months or years should mothers breastfeed their infants?
(5) Is manufactured baby milk just as good as mother's milk?
(6) Do you think that breastfed babies are healthier than bottle-fed babies?
(7) At what age should babies begin eating regular food?

OPEN TO DEBATE 2

UNIT 16

Sugar Daddies and Sugar Babies

Da-Hye: Hey Michael. I've heard that you have a girlfriend now.

Michael: Yeah, it's true. I've been dating another professor who's from Australia.

Da-Hye: I heard that she's a lot younger than you.

Michael: Well, that depends on how you define "a lot younger." She's actually eight years younger than me.

Da-Hye: I see. Well, that's not such a wide age gap.

Michael: Not at all. My father was 10 years older than my mother, and they've always had a happy marriage.

Da-Hye: I see. Well, I think that I would want my husband to be no more than 4-5 years older than me.

Michael: Well, you might change your mind if you met a really nice man who's a bit older.

Da-Hye: Yeah, I guess it could happen.

You two look like a "sugar daddy-sugar baby" couple!

What are you talking about? I don't even like sugar! There's no reason for me to be called a "sugar daddy."

I don't like sugar either! Can't you see that I'm as slim as chopsticks? I'm not a sugar baby. We're just in love, SWEET LOVE!

UNIT 16 — Sugar Daddies and Sugar Babies

One Tuesday night, around 11:00 pm, Amanda, who is a senior at Princeton University, received a text message from Stephen, a 60-year-old banker on Wall Street. He wanted Amanda to join him at his apartment in New York City immediately. Amanda responded that it was simply too late, and no trains were running. Stephen said that wouldn't be a problem; he would just send a limousine to pick her up. Amanda agreed on the condition that she could be back on campus in time to attend her 10:00 am class the next day. The evening went well. They had dinner at an expensive restaurant and then returned to Stephen's apartment for some intimate relations. After that, Amanda got back in the limo and had just enough time to arrive at her morning class.

The relationship of Stephen and Amanda is one that is often described as a "sugar daddy-sugar baby" relationship. The sugar daddy provides financial support and security, even paying for college tuition and offering a credit card. The sugar baby provides warmth, companionship, and intimate relations. How do such couples get together? Many of them do it through a website called "Seeking Arrangement." The site advertises that "mutually beneficial relationships" can be obtained in which young women shower rich men with attention, and young women get to enjoy the finer things of life, including fancy dinners, luxurious vacations, and monthly allowances. The website claims to have more than 300,000 registered members, and there are 10 times more sugar babies than sugar daddies.

Critics call this type of arrangement nothing more than just another form of prostitution. Brandon Wade, the founder of Seeking Arrangement responds to the criticism by saying, "We stress relationships that are mutually beneficial. We ask people to really think about what they want in a relationship and what they have to offer. That kind of upfront honesty is a good basis for any relationship."

What do you think?

(1) Are you shocked by the sugar daddy-sugar baby arrangement? Do you think of it as being immoral?
(2) Does the sugar daddy-sugar baby type of arrangement exist in your country? Is it legal or illegal?
(3) If you see an older man with a young woman, do you usually assume that they have a sugar daddy-sugar baby relationship?
(4) Have you heard about any older woman-younger man relationships (often called "cougar-cub" relationships)?
(5) Do you know any married couples who have a wide age difference? What is their marriage like?
(6) What is the maximum age difference that you would allow for your marriage partner?
(7) Some young couples want to "save themselves" and not sleep together until their honeymoon. Do you think that's wise or even possible?

OPEN TO DEBATE 2

UNIT 17

Legalization of Marijuana?

Ava: Hyun-Woo, are you familiar with the Korean laws about drugs?

Hyun-Woo: Well, I know a little. Why? Do you have a question?

Ava: Yes, I do. A friend of mine, who is from Canada, has been arrested for possession of marijuana.

Hyun-Woo: Oh my! That's not good. What happened?

Ava: Well, he went to a dance club last Saturday night, and one of his friends gave him a small quantity of marijuana.

Hyun-Woo: Uh-oh. He should never have accepted that.

Ava: Yeah, you're right. He was caught outside the club by Korean police and was arrested.

Hyun-Woo: And now he's in jail?

Ava: Yes, and I just wonder what's going to happen to him now.

Hyun-Woo: Korean laws are strict. He could be jailed for five years and fined $50,000.

Ava: Wow! That's very severe!

Hyun-Woo: Yeah, but since he's a foreign citizen, he will probably just be deported back to his home country.

It should be legalized right now!

No way! It should be illegal because it makes people helpless and hopeless!

Leave me alone! What matters is that I should be used PROPERLY. If well used, I can save a lot of people from painful suffering. But if I am abused, the side effects are devastating!

UNIT 17 — Legalization of Marijuana?

In most countries, marijuana, also called cannabis, has been considered an illegal drug since the 1930s, when it first began to be prohibited. However, in some jurisdictions, marijuana has recently been legalized, or "decriminalized." Possession of marijuana is legal in the Netherlands, Uruguay, and in the U.S. states of Colorado, Oregon, Alaska, and Washington, as well as several American cities. In addition, some countries allow for the medicinal use of marijuana, including Canada, the Czech Republic, and Israel. Among other countries, the level of strictness of marijuana laws varies greatly, from the least restrictive countries, such as Germany, Spain, and Jamaica, to the most restrictive, such as Malaysia, South Korea, and Saudi Arabia.

In the U.S. State of Colorado, where 55% of citizens voted to legalize marijuana in 2012, the effects of decriminalization began to mount. While arrests for possession of marijuana became a non-issue, other unintended side effects were noticeable. These effects included arrests for marijuana-intoxicated driving, increased use by teens, more emergency visits to the hospital, the rising economic dependence of Colorado counties and cities on the marijuana industry, and the illegal transportation of marijuana from Colorado into other states. In fact, Nebraska and Oklahoma, two nearby states, filed lawsuits against Colorado because their law enforcement burden was increased by the legalization in Colorado.

Meanwhile, arrests for marijuana possession and use continued in stricter jurisdictions. In 2014, a total of 37 English teachers in South Korea were arrested and booked on charges of selling and using marijuana. Among the arrestees were a South Korean citizen and a Korean-American who had brought two kilograms of marijuana into South Korea by using the U.S. military mail system. The two sold the marijuana to 32 different buyers, netting a profit of $107,716. South Korean law states that individuals caught using marijuana can be sentenced to a maximum of five years in jail or fined up to $50,000.

What do you think?

(1) Should marijuana possession and use be legalized in your country?
(2) If marijuana possession should remain illegal, what penalty should one face if found guilty?
(3) Do you think marijuana use is just as harmful as using harder drugs such as cocaine and heroin?
(4) Do you consider alcohol a drug? Which is worse, using marijuana or using alcohol?
(5) If someone wanted to buy marijuana in your country, where would they go?
(6) Do you know anyone who has tried marijuana? What did they say about it?
(7) If you traveled to a country with liberal marijuana laws, would you be interested in trying marijuana?

UNIT 18

The Blame for Internet Spam

Su-Yeon: Brandon, may I have your email address?

Brandon: Well, maybe. Why do you want my email address?

Su-Yeon: Oh, just for personal communication. Sometimes our class has an event, and we'd like to invite you.

Brandon: Okay. That sounds legitimate. I'll give it to you. I'm just cautious because I'm afraid of getting more spam emails.

Su-Yeon: Oh, I know what you mean. I detest that kind of email. I must get 20 spam emails per day.

Brandon: Only 20? I probably get 50 or so.

Su-Yeon: Have you tried getting a new email address?

Brandon: Yes, of course, but after a while, spammers seem to find out about my new address, and I have the same problem all over again.

Su-Yeon: Well, I know what you mean. I guess we are just stuck with this problem.

Brandon: Yeah, you're right. I just wish that the government would send all spammers to prison.

We have finally developed new technology that turns annoying spam emails into real Spam! So we welcome your spam emails 24/7. The more spam emails you send, the more Spam we can produce. We can solve both the problem of the worldwide food shortage and the problem of spam emails at the same time.

UNIT 18 — The Blame for Internet Spam

Do you know the name Alan Ralsky? Maybe not, but if you have been using the Internet for many years, you may have received some junk emails that he sent. Ralksy was one of the most prolific purveyors of Internet spam around the world. Unlike most spammers, who prefer to remain hidden, Ralsky was willing to give interviews to various newspapers. Actually, he claimed to be a commercial emailer and not a spammer. He also alleged that his business of commercial emailing complied with all laws. The courts did not believe Ralsky's claim that he was a legitimate commercial emailer, and he was eventually convicted of spamming and other fraudulent activities in June 2009. He was sentenced to four years and three months in prison, and he was fined $250,000. He was released from prison in 2012.

Ralsky is just one of many shameless spammers who flood our email accounts with unsolicited emails for dubious products. According to research conducted in 2014, there is an average of 54 billion spam messages sent every day. In that year, the number one topic of spam was pharmaceutical drugs, such as Viagra. Other popular topics were jobs with easy cash and diet products. According to Spamhaus.org, as of June 2016, the ten worst spam-enabling countries are the following, beginning with the worst: the United States, China, Russian Federation, Ukraine, Japan, Hong Kong, United Kingdom, Brazil, Germany, and India.

Why does spam continue to plague the Internet? Spamhaus.org provides the answer: It is because "a small number of Internet Service Providers knowingly sell service to professional spammers for profit." These ISPs "knowingly provide service to spam gangs and ignore spam reports from anti-spam systems and Internet users. In the name of profits, these networks turn a blind eye to blatant spam gangs on their networks."

What do you think?

(1) How many spam emails do you receive in a day?
(2) Have you taken any practical steps to block spam from entering your email inbox?
(3) What is the most common product promoted by the spam emails that you receive?
(4) Have you ever actually bought a product advertised in a spam email? What was it?
(5) Have any of your legitimate emails ever appeared accidentally in your spam box?
(6) Have you ever opened a spam email and received a virus from it?
(7) What are the worst deficiencies of the Internet, and what are its greatest benefits?

OPEN TO DEBATE 2

UNIT 19

Same-Sex Marriage

Jane: Jae-Ho, I read that a gay couple tried to get married in Korea.

Jae-Ho: Oh, you must be referring to Kim JhoGwang-soo and Kim Seung-hwan.

Jane: One is a film director, and the other is head of a movie company?

Jae-Ho: Yeah, that's right. They held a wedding ceremony in 2013 and tried to register their marriage.

Jane: What happened? Was their registration accepted?

Jae-Ho: No, not at all. Their application was rejected, and they filed a lawsuit, which was also dismissed.

Jane: What do you think Korea will do about the issue of same-sex marriage?

Jae-Ho: Well, Korea is still pretty conservative. It could take years for such unions to be legalized.

What counts in marriage is loving each other, respecting each other, and understanding each other, regardless of whether the union is between a man and a woman, a man and a man, or a woman and a woman. Marriage is a gift from god. When he gave us this gift, he never mentioned who should marry whom.

UNIT 19 Same-Sex Marriage

One of the most controversial issues in modern times has been that of same-sex marriage, also known as gay marriage. The first country to legalize such marriages was the Netherlands, in 2001. Since then, many advanced countries have established laws that permit same-sex marriages, including Argentina, Belgium, Brazil, Canada, France, Ireland, Norway, Portugal, South Africa, Spain, and Sweden.

In the United States, the road to legalization of same-sex marriages took numerous steps. The movement for civil marriage rights began in the 1970s, but appeals for same-sex unions were rejected for many years. In 1993, the Hawaii Supreme Court overturned Hawaii's ban against such unions. In 1996, in an attempt to return to a conservative view, the U.S. Congress passed a law called the Defense of Marriage Act (DOMA), which defined marriage solely as the union between a man and a woman. However, in 2004, Massachusetts became the first U.S. state to officially legalize same-sex marriage. Meanwhile, the momentum for permitting same-sex marriage steadily gained support, and in 2011, polls showed that a majority of Americans supported it. On May 9, 2012, President Barack Obama stated, "I think same-sex couples should be able to get married," and he supported the full repeal of the DOMA. In 2013, the U.S. Supreme Court ruled that the DOMA provisions about marriage were unconstitutional, and in 2015, the Court ruled that all state-level bans of same-sex marriage were likewise unconstitutional. This ruling effectively legalized same-sex marriage throughout the United States.

In spite of polls showing that almost 60% of Americans support legalizing same-sex marriage, conservative and religious groups continue to argue that allowing same-sex unions is wrong. These groups argue that children have a natural desire to be with their biological parents, children need both fathers and mothers, and evidence about the effects of parenting by same-sex couples is inadequate.

What do you think?

(1) What is the status of same-sex marriages in your country?
(2) Do you think that same-sex marriages should be allowed for gay people, or should they be permitted to have only "civil unions" or "domestic partnerships"?
(3) Have there been any TV shows or films in your country that feature gay characters?
(4) Do you know of any famous gay people in your country?
(5) Do you think a gay person could get elected to a political office in your country?
(6) Do you have any gay friends? Would you attend their wedding if invited?
(7) How would you respond if one of your family members announced that he/she was gay?

OPEN TO DEBATE 2

UNIT 20

Transgender Restrooms

Dae-Ho: Abigail, have you been following the debate about transgender restrooms?

Abigail: Yes, I have actually. It's been a big topic in the news recently.

Dae-Ho: What do you think about this issue?

Abigail: I think that people should use the toilet that matches their gender identity.

Dae-Ho: But what if some creepy guy dresses up like a woman just so he can enter the girls' toilet?

Abigail: Well, critics always bring up that issue, but actually, there are no examples of that happening. It's not a real issue.

Dae-Ho: I see. Well, here in Korea, we aren't really faced with this issue, so it seems strange to us.

Abigail: I understand, but Koreans should get prepared. The issue of transgender toilets will eventually become an issue here.

Dae-Ho: Yeah, I guess you're right.

You can't use this restroom! You're a man!

Get out! You're a woman! You're not allowed in here!

This is ridiculous! How long must I wait until the government decides which restroom I can use? This should be a very simple matter to resolve. I was born a man but look like a woman. So it should be okay for me to use either restroom as I please.

UNIT 20 Transgender Restrooms

In recent years, there has been a continuing debate in the United States concerning the rights of transgender individuals. In the U.S., the actual classification of a person's sex as male, female, or transgender is considered part of the states' jurisdiction and not a federal matter. As a result, the fifty states vary in their degree of acceptance and classification of transgender people. In connection with this issue, there naturally arises the question as to which restroom a transgender person should use. Restrooms are normally segregated by gender, though occasionally some facilities are designated as "unisex."

In mid-2016, the administration of President Barack Obama issued federal guidelines stating that schools throughout the country should allow transgender students to use restrooms, locker-rooms, and other facilities that match their gender identities. A number of states rejected these guidelines and filed a lawsuit in federal court against the new guidelines. In addition, some states, such as North Carolina, even passed "restroom bills" that required all individuals to use the restroom that matches the sex that is listed on their birth certificate. Advocates for transgender rights argued that such a law would require a person who was born as a man but now identifies as a woman to enter the men's room, wearing a dress and, for all practical purposes, being indistinguishable from a woman. The debate over this issue is likely to continue for an extended period before a solution is found.

What do you think?

(1) Do you agree with the view that a person should use the restroom that matches their gender identity?
(2) What problems could arise if everyone is required to use the restrooms that match the sex on their birth certificate?
(3) Would changing all toilets to individual rooms and designating them as unisex solve the problem?
(4) Do you have any transgender friends or acquaintances?
(5) Do you know of any famous transgender persons?
(6) Why would someone want to become transgender?
(7) Do you think that counseling could change the minds of persons who feel that they are transgender?

OPEN TO DEBATE 2

UNIT 21

Asian-Americans: Facing Discrimination?

Gabriel: Hey Ye-Eun! I heard that you were accepted at Seoul National University.

Ye-Eun: I guess news travels fast. Yes, it's true. I got my acceptance confirmation two days ago.

Gabriel: How did you manage to get into such a great school?

Ye-Eun: I worked very hard in high school, including many hours of after-school study.

Gabriel: Well, your hard work paid off.

Ye-Eun: I think that it helped that my father graduated from Seoul National. Maybe I got a few points for that.

Gabriel: Yeah. That's probably true, but still, the most important reason was your hard work.

Ye-Eun: I guess so. In any case, I'm very happy about it, and so are my parents.

Gabriel: Yeah, I'm sure they're proud of you. Many congrats on your accomplishment!

Ye-Eun: Thanks!

UNIT 21 — Asian-Americans: Facing Discrimination?

Michael Wang is a young Asian-American who had his heart set on attending an Ivy League university. His grade point average in high school was 4.67, and his score of 2230 on the SAT placed him in the 99th percentile of students who took the exam. For extracurricular activities, he participated in national competitions in the areas of speech, debate, and math. He also learned to play the piano well and even performed in the choir that sang at President Barack Obama's inauguration in 2008. With these great accomplishments under his belt, he applied to seven Ivy League universities and to Stanford University in 2013. Unfortunately, he was rejected by all of them, except for the University of Pennsylvania, leaving him completely demoralized. However, he didn't stop there. He filed a complaint with the U.S. Department of Education, claiming that Yale, Princeton, and Stanford discriminated against him because of his ethnic background as an Asian-American. Meanwhile, he ended up attending Williams College, a top liberal arts college but not one of the Ivies.

Wang is not the only Asian-American who feels discriminated against. More than 60 Asian groups have joined forces in a lawsuit against Harvard University and other Ivy League universities, alleging that those institutions use racial quotas for admissions purposes. In other words, the applicants claim that the universities seek to accept a certain percentage of white Americans, African-Americans, Latino-Americans, and Asian-Americans. The result of this policy is that Asian-American applicants may be rejected, even though they have higher qualifications.

In response to such criticisms, Harvard University responded that it maintains a "holistic admissions process" and seeks to build a diverse class of incoming students. As part of that commitment, Harvard stated that its most recent incoming freshmen class included the following minorities: 21.1% Asian-American, 13% Hispanic/Latino, 11.6% African-American, and 1.5% Native American/Pacific Islander. Furthermore, Harvard stated that previous government investigations concluded that Harvard's admission policies were fully compliant with federal law.

What do you think?

(1) Do you think that Wang was discriminated against because he is Asian-American?
(2) Asian-Americans comprise about 5% of the U.S. population, yet Harvard's freshman class had 21.1% Asian-Americans. Isn't that enough?
(3) How do students in your country get into the top universities—through their accomplishments or because of other factors, such as wealth or privilege?
(4) What are the top five universities in your country? Do you know anyone who attended one of them?
(5) How much does it cost to attend the top university in your country?
(6) Do you have any friends or acquaintances who attended an Ivy League school?
(7) Can you name all eight Ivy League universities?

OPEN TO DEBATE 2

UNIT 22

Eating Live Animals

Hailey: Min-Soo, I hear that your English class is going out for dinner tonight.

Min-Soo: Yeah, we are. Would you like to join us?

Hailey: That depends. What kind of restaurant are you going to?

Min-Soo: A seafood restaurant. We're going to have *sannakji*.

Hailey: *Sannakji*? Isn't that the small live octopus?

Min-Soo: Yes, that's right. It's a sort of delicacy in Korea.

Hailey: Well, I'm afraid that I cannot imagine ever eating a living thing.

Min-Soo: That's okay. If you don't want to eat it, you can choose another kind of seafood.

Hailey: Hmmm... actually, I'm not a big fan of seafood anyway. I think I should skip this time.

Min-Soo: Okay. No problem. We can try something different next time.

Humans don't know that they should only eat octopus in the water. That's why they sometimes choke to death when they eat live octopus.

Live frog is the best dish in the world! I'm afraid that humans have discovered this too! If they know that live frogs are healthy and tasty, my species will go extinct ... as I'm about to!

I'm sick and tired of eating live mice! Roasted mice would be much tastier. Unfortunately, I don't know how to make fire!

UNIT 22 — Eating Live Animals

A recent graphic video clip posted on youtube.com has caused shock around the world. The video shows several live baby mice, squirming around in a sauce. A Chinese man picks up a baby mouse with his chopsticks, pops it into his mouth, and eats it alive. Such a practice seems unsettling and deranged to many people, especially to those who live in Western countries. However, the custom of eating live animals is not as rare as one might think. In some countries, small animals, such as octopus, frogs, and fish, are eaten alive.

In Korea, many residents enjoy a dish of live octopus called *sannakji*. A small octopus, called *nakji*, is cut into small pieces while still alive and served immediately, usually seasoned with sesame oil. The legs of the octopus are still squirming on the plate as the diners consume them. The dish can also be served with the whole octopus intact. *Sannakji* is served in restaurants that specialize in raw fish and as a side dish in bars where *soju*, a Korean alcohol, is served. Because the suction cups on the arms of the octopuses are still active while being ingested, *sannakji* can easily become a choking hazard for diners, especially for those who are intoxicated. In 2008, a man in Gwangju, Korea, almost died when he choked on an octopus leg.

The custom of eating live animals is practiced in a number of countries. In Japan, sashimi is made from live seafood, most often fish. The fish is usually filleted without being killed and served while its heart is still beating and its mouth opening and closing. Some Japanese and Chinese citizens have been known to eat frog sashimi. A live frog is stabbed and skinned in front of a diner, with the frog's beating heart left on the plate. In China, a dish called *yin yang fish* is prepared by quickly deep-frying a fish while the head is still fresh and moving.

What do you think?

(1) Is the practice of eating live animals cruel and barbaric or simply a matter of cultural relativism?
(2) Have you ever eaten a living thing, such as *sannakji*? What was it like?
(3) What is the most unusual food that you have ever heard of?
(4) What is the most unusual food that you have personally eaten?
(5) Do you like to eat raw fish? How often do you eat it?
(6) What is your favorite food of all time?
(7) How do you like a steak cooked: rare, medium rare, medium, medium well, well done?

UNIT 23

Cruelty to Animals

Brianna: Jung-Wook, do you have a pet?

Jung-Wook: Yes, I do actually. I have a dog.

Brianna: How long have you had it?

Jung-Wook: I received it as a birthday gift when I was eleven. It was just a puppy then, but now it's ten years old.

Brianna: Wow! You've had it for a long time. It must be very old in dog years.

Jung-Wook: Yeah, I guess so. It's like a senior citizen.

Brianna: Have you ever lost your temper with your dog?

Jung-Wook: When I was a kid, I did a few times, but I always tried to teach it the correct behavior. I have never hit my dog.

Brianna: That's good. That would be a case of animal abuse, which is incredibly sad.

Jung-Wook: I agree with you.

— I'm going to hit this vicious dog!
— You'd better think twice. If you hit it, you'll be arrested for cruelty to animals.
— Then what can I do about this mad dog biting me?
— Don't worry! We'll give him a warning.

Everybody is equal under the law.

UNIT 23 — Cruelty to Animals

In 2015, a 22-year-old woman named Hayley Cowan, who lived in the United Kingdom, owned a female Staffordshire bull terrier, which was named Beau. Apparently, Cowan became angry with Beau and kicked her in the face, leaving the dog injured. Some of Cowan's friends found out about the incident and took the dog away from her. After some time, the friends returned the dog to Cowan who promised not to hurt the dog again. Later, when friends visited Cowan, they noticed that Beau had disappeared, and the friends became worried about the dog. One friend looked into Cowan's garden and found Beau's remains. The friend immediately called the Royal Society for the Prevention of Cruelty to Animals (RSPCA) and reported the incident. The dog's body was examined by authorities, and it was determined that Beau had died from strangulation because duct tape had been wrapped around her muzzle.

Cowan was arrested for cruelty to animals. She later pled guilty to two counts of causing unnecessary suffering to animals, and she was sentenced to four months in prison. According to the U.K. Animal Welfare Act of 2006, a person is guilty of animal abuse if an act of the person, or a failure to act, causes an animal to suffer. If this occurs, the law allows for a maximum sentence of six months' imprisonment or a fine of £20,000. In Cowan's case, there was the extenuating claim that she suffered from mental health problems. As a result, she was given a sentence of four months' imprisonment, was fined £500 in court costs, and was disqualified from keeping an animal as a pet in the future.

The reaction of British citizens was largely critical of the court's decision. Many people believed that Cowan should have received a much longer prison sentence. Also, many citizens called for an increase in the penalties prescribed by the law for instances of animal cruelty.

What do you think?

(1) Do you think that the prison sentence given to Cowan was reasonable?
(2) Does your country have strong laws and penalties for animal cruelty?
(3) Does your country have an organization like the RSPCA whose purpose is to protect animals?
(4) Have you read about any cases of animal cruelty? What happened?
(5) If you saw someone harming an animal, would you try to intervene?
(6) What is the most popular type of pet in your country?
(7) If you could own any sort of pet, what would you choose?

OPEN TO DEBATE 2

UNIT 24

An Apology for Hiroshima?

Sung-Jin: Destiny, you are from the United States, right?

Destiny: Yeah, that's right.

Sung-Jin: I see that your president visited Hiroshima recently.

Destiny: Yes, that's right. President Obama was the first president to visit Hiroshima while he was still in office.

Sung-Jin: Did he offer any sort of apology for the bombing of Hiroshima?

Destiny: No, he didn't, but he gave an impassioned plea for an end to nuclear weapons.

Sung-Jin: Do you think he should have given an apology?

Destiny: I have mixed emotions about that question. There are good arguments for both sides.

Sung-Jin: I see. It's a very difficult issue.

Destiny: Yes, it is, but he called for the elimination of all nuclear weapons, which I could certainly agree with.

Sung-Jin: Me too.

— I feel so bad that we're dropping this nuclear bomb. So many people are going to die or suffer from radioactivity.
— You don't have to be sorry! This is the only way to end this dreadful war, and we have to follow the commander-in-chief's orders. Besides, Japan started the war!

UNIT 24 — An Apology for Hiroshima?

On May 8, 1945, Nazi Germany surrendered, marking the end of World War II in Europe. However, the war still raged in the Pacific area, and Japan showed little sign of surrender. In order to hasten the end of the war, on August 6, 1945, the United States dropped the first nuclear bomb ever on the city of Hiroshima, Japan. About 16 hours after the bomb fell, President Harry S. Truman called on Japan to surrender, warning them to "expect a rain of ruin from the air, the like of which has never been seen on this earth." Three days later, on August 9, the U.S. dropped another nuclear bomb on the city of Nagasaki. The effects of the atomic bombs were devastating. Approximately 140,000 people died in Hiroshima and about 80,000 in Nagasaki. The massive number of victims included about 50,000 Koreans who had been forced into labor in Japan. About half the deaths occurred immediately, and the rest occurred during the following months as people died from burns, radiation sickness, and other injuries. In both cities, most of the dead were civilians, although some military personnel were killed in Hiroshima, which held a large military garrison.

To this day, people around the world, including Americans, debate the issue of whether it was necessary to wreak such havoc on the Japanese population in order to end the war. Supporters of the bombings argue that they saved half a million American lives and even many Japanese lives that would have been lost in an invasion. Opponents argue that the nuclear bombs were fundamentally immoral and that the war could have been won through other means.

On May 27, 2016, President Barack Obama became the first sitting president to visit Hiroshima. While Obama did not apologize for the bombing of Hiroshima, he called on the world to put an end to nuclear weapons.

What do you think?

(1) Do you think the nuclear bombings were necessary to end the war quickly?
(2) How would the war have ended if the nuclear bombs were not dropped?
(3) Should President Obama have apologized to the Japanese people for the bombings?
(4) Do you think your country should have access to nuclear weapons?
(5) Experts say that eight countries possess nuclear weapons. How many of them can you name?
(6) How would you rank the possibility that another nuclear war might break out?
(7) Do you know anyone who fought in a war? Does that person ever talk about their experience?

OPEN TO DEBATE 2

UNIT 25

Fur Coats

Chris: Wow! So-Yun, that's a beautiful fur coat. What kind of fur is it?

So-Yun: It's mink. I received it as a gift when I visited my aunt in New York.

Chris: Well, that's nice. I hear that fur coats cost over $1,000.

So-Yun: Maybe that's true, but my aunt had already worn this one for a few years.

Chris: Well, it still looks in good condition. She took good care of it.

So-Yun: Yeah, that's one of the problems with fur coats. You must follow strict rules for taking care of them.

Chris: What kind of rules?

So-Yun: During hot weather, fur coats have to be stored at seven degrees Celsius and 50% humidity.

Chris: How can you maintain that temperature in your home?

So-Yun: I can't. I have to leave the coat with a professional storage service, which is expensive.

Chris: Wow! I had no idea it was so complicated to own a fur coat.

So-Yun: Well, it's difficult, and I also have to hear ethical objections to fur coats from my friends.

UNIT 25   Fur Coats

On February 19, 2016, the London Fashion Week opened with great fanfare. However, there was one significant distraction: three female models protested the opening of the exhibition by carrying signs that said "FUR IS TOXIC." They were nearly nude, wearing nothing but panties, tape over their breasts, and gas masks. The protestors had teamed up with the activist organization People for the Ethical Treatment of Animals. PETA associate director Elisa Allen stated, "There's nothing fashionable about fur torn from the bodies of struggling animals and then laden with chemicals that are dangerous to people who wear it. PETA is urging kind people to choose fur-free clothing for the sake of their own health and animal welfare."

Is it morally acceptable to wear a fur coat? Natasha de Young, age 27, says yes, according to the British newspaper *Daily Mail*. She remembers fondly the mink coats that her mother wore in a glamorous manner, making her look like a movie star. Later, Natasha wore her own fur coats and said, "I've never had a moral problem wearing mink because it wasn't an endangered species. Most people eat meat and wear leather, so what's the difference?"

Others argue that wearing fur clothing is inhumane and unethical. When foxes and minks are trapped for their fur, the animals often chew off their own arms and legs to free themselves from the traps. In the case of animals that are bred in captivity for their fur, only the fur is used, and the rest of the animal's body is just thrown away. Some of these animals are skinned alive. Also, fake fur looks just as good as real fur. When you wear a false fur, you don't have to worry about wearing the coat of a dead animal around your body. Finally, teaching your children that fur is wrong will help them become compassionate human beings.

What do you think?

(1) Is it morally acceptable to wear animal fur, or is it a cruel practice that should be banned?
(2) Is there a large fur clothing industry in your country? What kinds of fur products are made?
(3) How much would a fur coat cost in your country?
(4) Do you personally own any clothing made from fur? Do you know anyone who does?
(5) Would you accept a piece of fur clothing as a gift?
(6) Have you ever personally killed an animal? What happened?
(7) Do you eat meat every day? Have you ever skipped eating meat for a day?

OPEN TO DEBATE 2

UNIT 26

Discrimination against Muslims

Emily: Chan-Woo, I need your help.

Chan-Woo: Yes, of course. What can I do?

Emily: In our English class tomorrow, we will be welcoming a new student.

Chan-Woo: Well, that sounds great. I always enjoy meeting new people.

Emily: Good. Our new student is from Iran, and she is a Muslim, and she will probably be wearing a traditional type of head covering.

Chan-Woo: That's cool. I'll look forward to meeting her.

Emily: Great. Well, I am going to ask you to make an extra effort to be friendly and to make her feel welcome.

Chan-Woo: Of course. I already have two Muslim friends from my high school. I'll be happy to be her friend.

Emily: That's wonderful. We want all our students to feel appreciated and welcome.

Appearance has nothing to do with our character. We're all humans! So there is no reason to discriminate against each other. Remember the words of Martin Luther King, Jr.: People should not be judged by the color of their skin, but by the content of their character.

UNIT 26 — Discrimination against Muslims

On December 11, 2015, an American man named Gill Parker Payne, age 37, of Gastonia, North Carolina, boarded a flight from Chicago to Albuquerque, New Mexico. Toward the end of the flight, he saw a Muslim woman, a few rows in front of him, who was wearing a traditional type of scarf called a hijab. He became enraged, rushed forward toward the woman, and screamed, "Take it off! This is America!" Then he immediately pulled the hijab off the woman's head. The woman, who was identified only as K.A. in news reports, felt violated and quickly put her hijab back on. When the plane landed in Albuquerque, Payne was arrested. Later, in his court appearance, he pleaded guilty to a misdemeanor hate crime, admitting that he forcefully removed the victim's hijab and obstructed the free exercise of her religious beliefs. Because Payne confessed, he was sentenced to two months of home detention and a period of probation.

The assault and indignity that K.A. suffered at the hands of Payne was only the tip of the iceberg in a massive surge in anti-Muslim rhetoric and Islamophobic hate crimes in the United States during that year. Research shows that the year 2015 saw the highest level of anti-Muslim sentiment since 2001. American Muslims continued to face widespread discrimination, harassment, and violence. A similar upsurge of hate crimes against Muslims happened in the U.K. as well. According to the Metropolitan Police of London, England, such crimes have spiked dramatically in recent years.

In response to Payne's hate crime, a spokesperson for the U.S. Department of Justice stated, "No matter what one's faith is, all Americans are entitled to peacefully exercise their religious beliefs free from discrimination and violence. Using or threatening force against individuals because of their religion is an affront to the fundamental values of this nation. The Civil Rights Division will continue to be vigilant in protecting the religious liberties guaranteed to all Americans."

What do you think?

(1) Payne did not receive any jail time for his crime. Do you think this was fair?
(2) Why do you think Muslims have become targets of discrimination?
(3) Are there many Muslims in your country? Do they face discrimination because of their religion?
(4) Do you have any friends who are Muslims? How did you meet them?
(5) Would you consider marrying a person of the Muslim faith? Why or why not?
(6) Have you ever traveled to a Muslim-majority country? What was it like?
(7) Have you ever felt discriminated against because of your religion or ethnic origin?

OPEN TO DEBATE 2

UNIT 27

Once a Cheater, Always a Cheater?

Jonathan: Min-Ju, you look so sad today. What's wrong?

Min-Ju: Oh, Jonathan, I think I have a problem. I think my boyfriend is cheating on me.

Jonathan: That's terrible. Why do you think he's cheating?

Min-Ju: I saw him sitting in a coffee shop yesterday, and he was talking in a charming way to a pretty girl.

Jonathan: Well, there could be a totally innocent explanation for that. Maybe she's an old friend or a relative.

Min-Ju: I guess that could be true. I just don't know.

Jonathan: Before you jump to conclusions, why don't you just ask him about that girl? Maybe there's a completely legitimate explanation.

Min-Ju: Okay. I will do that. Thanks for your advice.

Jonathan: No problem. Please let me know how it turns out.

― So finally, I've caught you red-handed! You're having a love affair! I'm going to kill you!
― Oh, please calm down! It's not my fault! I have a gene that "forces" me to have love affairs. I can't help myself!
― So, you blame it on your gene? Well, that gives me a good excuse too. If I kill you, it's my gene that forced me to kill you. I'll be innocent!

I hope the bullet won't pass through him and hit me too!

UNIT 27 — Once a Cheater, Always a Cheater?

According to a study produced at the University of Chicago, 22% of married men and 15% of married women have cheated at least once. Thus, cheating is a fairly common occurrence, and many people believe the old axiom that says, "Once a cheater, always a cheater." This saying means that, if your partner cheats on you, they are very likely to cheat again, so you can never trust them again. But is it really true? According to clinical psychiatrist Richard Reid, who is a specialist in relationship issues, "It's simplistic to suggest that everyone who has had an affair will definitely cheat again. While some people's personalities are certainly predisposed towards repeat behavior, the vast majority of affairs happen because people are emotionally overwhelmed and under-resourced to properly acknowledge and address their negative feelings." Reid claims that people do not cheat because of a sudden lapse in judgment. They cheat because they have some emotional turmoil in their life. If a person can understand their motivations for cheating, those motivations can be dealt with, and the cheating behavior can be stopped.

On the other hand, some scientists claim that there is actually a scientific reason for the fact that some people cheat, and others don't. It is known that dopamine, a pleasure-centered hormone in the human body, is released after exercise, eating delicious food, and other enjoyable experiences, and this hormone plays a big role in whether a person is likely to cheat. Research shows that, if nature has given you a long allele variant of the dopamine receptor in your body, you are more than twice as likely to cheat than if you have been given a short allele variant. (An allele is a form of a gene that is responsible for hereditary variation.)

What do you think?

(1) Do you think this saying is true: "Once a cheater, always a cheater"?
(2) Do you agree with the view that cheating may be caused to some degree by genetics?
(3) What activities besides sleeping with another person could be considered cheating?
(4) Has anyone ever cheated on you? Did you catch them lying about it?
(5) If your partner cheated but felt remorse, could you forgive them, or would you end the relationship?
(6) Do you think it's true that, if one person makes a lot of money, that person is more likely to cheat on a partner?
(7) Do you think that cheating in marriage, which is called adultery, should be classified as a criminal offense?

OPEN TO DEBATE 2

UNIT 28

Finding Mr./Ms. Right

Kang-Dae: Ella, could I ask you a personal question?

Ella: Of course, as long as it's not too personal.

Kang-Dae: Well, you and Karl seem to be a very happy couple. You've been married for more than five years, right?

Ella: Yes, that's right. We've been married for almost six years, and we are very happy together.

Kang-Dae: Well, this is my question: Were you searching for a "Mr. Right" when you met Karl?

Ella: No, I wasn't actually. I just dated the guys who happened to be available and interested in me when I was in college.

Kang-Dae: I see. Well, did you think Karl was your Mr. Right?

Ella: Not at first. We had to take a long time to get to know each other. Also, I always remembered a piece of advice that my grandmother gave me.

Kang-Dae: What sort of advice?

Ella: She said, "You will never find a partner who meets 100% of what you want, and you are not likely 100% of what someone else would like."

Kang-Dae: Well, that sounds like very sound advice.

In spite of our prenup, I will love her forever. She's always been my soul mate and always will be!

I wasn't sure he was my Mr. Right. That's why I demanded we have a prenup. It'll ensure that my rights are guaranteed.

Prenuptial agreements are necessary because we don't know who is Mr. Right or Ms. Right unless we live together for a long time. But some say the fact that we make a prenuptial agreement really means that we ARE ALWAYS READY to part ways. That's our dilemma.

UNIT 28 — Finding Mr./Ms. Right

Many young people conduct their romantic lives as though there is only one "Mr. Right/Ms. Right" for them. However, some scientists have recently claimed that research shows that you should not live in hope of meeting the perfect partner. It's actually better to settle for "Mr./Ms. Right Now" than to wait for a perfect "Mr./Ms. Right" in the future. These researchers say that human nature has evolved by taking safe bets in relationships and by having risk-aversion behavior.

In support of this notion, Chris Adami, Professor of Microbiology at Michigan State University, conducted research using a computational model populated with digital organisms. The research team traced risk-taking behaviors through thousands of generations of the organisms. The scientists concluded that early humans were forced to make a choice between two distinct possibilities: (1) Should they mate with a nearby and available companion, even though that companion was potentially inferior and would produce inferior offspring? or (2) Should they wait for Mr./Ms. Perfect to appear later? Professor Adami argued that, if they chose to wait for the perfect partner, they ran the risk of never mating. Thus, nature evolved to opt for the "safest bet," and it became wise to "settle" early for the best partner that was available. In support of Adami's thesis is the fact that people who are raised in small groups, for example, smaller than 150 people, tend to avoid risk in relationships much more than those who are raised in a larger community. In fact, according to biologists, early humans lived in small groups, consisting of about 150 individuals.

On the other hand, Professor Adami admitted that human beings do not all evolve to be the same and that it is clear that not everyone develops the same level of risk-aversion. As a result, there is a huge diversity of levels of risk acceptance, and some people are more likely to take risks than others.

What do you think?

(1) Do you believe that somewhere there is a perfect match for every human being?
(2) Are you searching/did you search for your own perfect match?
(3) Do you know any couples that you think are perfectly matched?
(4) Do you know any couples that do not seem to be perfectly matched but who still manage to have a fulfilling relationship?
(5) Do you know any couples who appeared to be perfectly matched but who eventually broke up?
(6) There's an old saying about romance that states, "Opposites attract." Do you think it's true?
(7) Do you think your parents are/were a perfect match or did they just "settle" for each other?

OPEN TO DEBATE 2

UNIT 29

Bullying in Public Schools

Yu-Jin: Kevin, I need your advice.

Kevin: Well, I'm not very good at giving advice, but I will try.

Yu-Jin: My little brother is still in high school, and he's facing a problem with bullies.

Kevin: Oh, that's terrible! Has he been bullied physically or psychologically?

Yu-Jin: Mostly psychological. There are some other boys who call him bad names and tell him he's stupid.

Kevin: Incredible! Has anyone in your family talked to the school administrators?

Yu-Jin: Not yet. My parents work a lot and don't have much free time. I think that I'll have to be the one to talk to the school officials.

Kevin: Well, if you like, I can go along with you to meet them. I know a little bit about bullying, and I can certainly provide some moral support.

Yu-Jin: Thanks very much. I'll make an appointment next week and let you know the time.

Because online bullying has become such a serious social problem, Samsung has introduced a very innovative smart phone. With this phone, you can't post negative statements online while remaining anonymous. Also, Apple has announced it has developed new software technology that automatically turns negative statements into positive statements. Which one is better? Do you think these smart phones are selling well?

I'm better than you! I'll be selling like hotcakes!

Nonsense! Customers will decide which one is better. Time will tell!

UNIT 29: Bullying in Public Schools

March 31, 2016, should have been a happy day for Aileen Jiminian, age 17, a senior at the Manhattan Village Academy in New York City. She had recently become a semifinalist for the *New York Times* College Scholarship Program and seemed to have a bright future. She also had a twin sister who attended the same school. But Aileen had had all that she could take from classmates who bullied her, often calling her stupid or ugly or awkward. Aileen was so despondent that, during lunch hour, she left the school's campus and climbed onto the subway tracks at the 23rd Street Station on Seventh Avenue. Moments later, she was fatally struck by a train around 12:30 p.m. The school's administration and teachers told students that Aileen was in a "bad accident," and they should not talk about her or what happened. The school also sent a letter to students' parents informing them that Aileen had "passed away." In spite of the school's admonition not to talk about the incident, some students went to the school's grief counselor and confessed that they were feeling guilty because of the way they had mistreated Aileen.

The treatment of Aileen Jiminian is just one example of the devastating effects of bullying in public schools and the apparent indifference of many school administrators. Studies show that 77% of students have been bullied psychologically, verbally, or physically, and that 20% of students have admitted to doing some bullying themselves. To make matters worse, the advent of the Internet Age has opened a new forum for bullying: cyberbullying. Through interactive technologies, such as text messages, Twitter, and Facebook, cyberbullying can occur around the clock and take bullying to a new level of intensity. Sadly, 53% of students have confessed that they made mean or hurtful statements to another person online.

What do you think?

(1) Why would someone take their own life because of bullying?
(2) Do you think the school responded appropriately to the death of Aileen Jiminian?
(3) Have you witnessed any cases of bullying where you went to school? What happened?
(4) Have you ever been bullied yourself? What sort of bullying occurred?
(5) Has anyone ever made hurtful statements about you online? What did they say?
(6) Have you ever posted a negative statement online while remaining anonymous?
(7) What sort of punishment should high school bullies face?

OPEN TO DEBATE 2

UNIT 30

The Death of Marriage?

William: Ji-Min, what is the average age of Koreans when they get married?

Ji-Min: Well, as you can imagine, the average age has been increasing for the current generation.

William: Have you read any statistics about it?

Ji-Min: The last statistics that I saw are from 2014. The average age of the man was 32.4, and the woman was 29.8.

William: Oh, wow! That means that they are both around age 30.

Ji-Min: Yes, it's true, and in general, the man is usually a few years older than the woman.

William: Yeah, that's a traditional approach. Do you know of any couples who just live together without getting married?

Ji-Min: Yes, I know a girl from college who is living with her boyfriend.

William: I wonder if her parents know about it.

Ji-Min: Yes, they do, and they're cool with it, but most parents are not so open-minded.

William: I can imagine that the older generation is fairly conservative about that.

Ji-Min: Yes, that's true.

In 2050, Oxford University Press decides that it will erase two words in the dictionary: the words marriage and divorce. Why? Because no one gets married anymore nor do they get divorced.

UNIT 30 — The Death of Marriage?

On April 7, 2015, CNN reporter Carol Costello published an article at the CNN website with the ominous title "Ready for the Marriage Apocalypse?" The word apocalypse here refers to a dramatic change and upheaval in the future. According to Costello, the United States may become marriage-free in the future, with everyone living happily as singles. Costello interviewed a group of college students, and she was surprised by what they said about marriage. One young woman said frankly, "I didn't go to college for four years to be a mom. There's no housewife degree. I've worked my butt off for four years to get this degree. You want to use it. You want to be successful. You want to have that happy part of your life as well." Another young woman named Jackie agreed and added, "I don't think you need a wedding ring to prove that you love someone. I see a lot of people get married too soon, or they stay together and are unhappy because they are afraid to be alone. And I would rather be alone, successful, and happy than in a relationship where I'm not happy. ... I'm OK being single forever. As long as I'm happy."

The negative attitudes of the young women toward marriage are borne out by statistics. According to a Pew Research report, 50% of American respondents agreed with the idea that society is just as well off if people have priorities other than marriage and children. The lifestyles of Scandinavians seem to support this notion. Many Swedes, for example, believe that marriage often disappoints people because individuals have the unrealistic expectation that their partner will be a source of fulfillment for them. It's just better to remain single. Thus, in Norway, Sweden, and Denmark, more than 80% of couples have their first child out of wedlock. It's clear that the idea of marriage has become obsolete in parts of Scandinavia.

What do you think?

(1) Do you think that marriage is becoming an obsolete institution?
(2) What is your opinion of the Scandinavian attitude toward marriage?
(3) Why do you think more people are viewing marriage as an option, not a necessity?
(4) Do you agree that society is just as well off if people have priorities besides getting married and having children?
(5) Do you know any couples who had a baby before being married?
(6) Do you consider marriage a necessity for yourself?
(7) Would you ever consider having a baby while you're still single?

OPEN TO DEBATE 2

UNIT 31

Wealthy Pastors: Truly Serving God?

Liz: Hi Jae-Won. Could you help me with something?

Jae-Won: Sure Liz. What do you need help with?

Liz: I just moved to Korea, and I'm looking for a church, but I don't know anything about churches here.

Jae-Won: What denomination are you?

Liz: I'm Presbyterian, and I know there are a lot of Presbyterian churches in Korea.

Jae-Won: Yes, that's correct. We call the Presbyterian church *jangno-kyohoe* in Korean.

Liz: Is there a Presbyterian church near here?

Jae-Won: Well, there's a small one nearby, but I know where there's a huge one that you might prefer. The pastor is very famous.

Liz: Oh, actually, I prefer small churches. I feel lost in a big church.

Jae-Won: I see. Well, let me write down some directions for you to the small church.

I am the messenger of God! I'm always lobbying God to fulfill your wishes. But I need more money to do a good job.

I'm just 20. I don't need a ticket to heaven, but I want to be rich ASAP! How can I get a lot of money like you?

I'm dying. How much is a ticket to heaven? I'm willing to sell all my possessions!

UNIT 31
Wealthy Pastors: Truly Serving God?

November 24, 2014, was a sad day for the American pastor, Reverend Creflo Dollar. His private Gulfstream III jet ran off the runway at an airport in the United Kingdom. But Pastor Dollar knew a way to replace the damaged jet quickly. He simply asked his followers to pay $60 million for a new Gulfstream G650 jet, which was one of the fastest planes in existence at the time. Dollar suggested that each of his followers contribute $300 or more, and he would secure enough money to buy the plane. The American public was outraged, and Dollar ended the fundraising campaign. However, his ministry's website kept the project visible on the donation page. A few months later, the ministry announced that they were ready to purchase the new jet. Dollar is one of many American pastors who preach what is called "prosperity theology" or the "gospel of wealth." He claims that God intends to bless all Christians financially and that he should not be criticized for living such a lavish lifestyle that includes two Rolls-Royce automobiles, his private jet, and several houses worth millions of dollars.

Creflo Dollar is not the only wealthy pastor in the world. According to news reports, the richest pastor in the world is Edir Macedo, a Brazilian pastor whose net worth is estimated at $1.1 billion. When he is criticized for his massive wealth, he responds by saying, "If I preach prosperity and my clothes are ragged, who will follow me?" Then there is David Oyedepo, pastor of the Faith Tabernacle in Nigeria, which according to the *Guinness Book of World Records* has the largest church auditorium in the world, seating 50,000 people. Oyedepo is said to be worth $150 million, and he has a small fleet of four private jets. Two other Nigerian ministers also make the top-10 list of richest pastors: Enoch Adeboye, with a net worth of $55 million, and Chris Oyakhilome, with a net worth of $50 million.

What do you think?

(1) In your opinion, are these wealthy pastors truly serving God?
(2) Do you think of religion as a positive force in the world? If so, how does it help people?
(3) Are there any rich pastors in your country? How did they accumulate their wealth?
(4) Have you ever donated money to a religious institution? What did you think your donation would accomplish?
(5) Have you ever bought or read a book written by a pastor? What was it?
(6) Are there any missionaries in your country? Have you ever talked to any of them?
(7) Do you personally have a religion? How often do you visit a place of worship?

UNIT 32

Proliferation of Drones

Emma: Chin-Hae, have you heard the latest news?

Chin-Hae: I'm not sure. What news are you talking about?

Emma: The Korean government has said that it will allow restaurants to use 2-passenger compact electric vehicles to deliver food.

Chin-Hae: Well, that sounds good.

Emma: Also, the government will allow companies to use drones to transport packages and to advertise.

Chin-Hae: Hmmm... I'm not so sure I like that idea.

Emma: Why? Drones are high-tech and the wave of the future.

Chin-Hae: Well, I think drone technology is not developed enough yet. I think drones could crash into buildings or people.

Emma: Yeah, I guess that's possible.

Chin-Hae: I think the government needs to wait until more research is done that proves that drones are safe enough to be used in public spaces.

The proliferation of drones has made cars and airplanes obsolete. But even drones will become outdated in the next century. With the help of biology, men will have wings!

UNIT 32 Proliferation of Drones

One night in December 2015, Owen Ouyang, a Chinese exchange student living in California, decided to have some fun. He had recently purchased a new high-tech drone from an online vendor for $1,000. The manufacturer advertised that the drone was "easy to fly," and since it only weighed 2.8 pounds (1.3 kg), it should not create any problems. Unfortunately, Ouyang found it difficult to control the drone, and it flew upward to more than 700 feet, which placed it directly into the path of a California Highway Patrol helicopter. The pilot of the helicopter managed to avert disaster by making a sharp right-hand turn before the drone crashed into the helicopter.

Another interesting case shows the shocking effects of what we might call "drone rage." In October 2015, William H. Merideth, who lives in Hillview, Kentucky, noticed that a drone was hovering over his house. Merideth suspected that the drone was spying and taking pictures of his daughter, who was sunbathing in the back yard. Merideth took out a gun and shot the drone down. A neighbor called the police, who came promptly and investigated the incident. Later, the owner of the drone and three friends appeared at Merideth's house and demanded $1,800 to replace the drone. Merideth was holding a 40mm Glock pistol and told them, "If you cross my sidewalk, there's gonna be another shooting." Eventually, Merideth was charged with the crimes of "wanton endangerment" and "criminal mischief." However, a judge dismissed the charges, stating that Merideth's privacy was violated, and he had a right to shoot down the drone.

These shocking cases demonstrate the growing public concern about the dangers of recreational drones. One research group found that there were 327 "close encounters" between drones and manned aircraft in just a 21-month period. That number included 51 cases in which a drone came within 50 feet of a conventional aircraft. Legislators are continuing to wrestle with exactly how drones should be regulated.

What do you think?

(1) Do you think Merideth was justified in shooting down the drone?
(2) Have you heard similar horror stories about drones in your country?
(3) Are there any government restrictions placed on drone ownership and use in your country?
(4) Should individuals be allowed to own drones or should they be restricted to military and scientific use?
(5) Do you know anyone who owns a drone? Where do they fly it?
(6) Have you ever seen a drone flying above? What was your personal reaction?
(7) Would you personally like to own a drone? Why or why not?

OPEN TO DEBATE 2

UNIT 33

Future Foods

Anna: Min-Ho, what is the strangest thing that you have ever eaten?

Min-Ho: Hmmm.... maybe that would be some "silk worm pupae." We call it *bundaegi* in Korean.

Anna: Oh, I've seen that. No offense, but it looks and smells disgusting to me.

Min-Ho: Oh, I understand. A lot of Westerners would not dream of eating it.

Anna: Well, I did try it once.

Min-Ho: Oh, you were brave. What happened?

Anna: A Korean friend of mine bought one cup of *bundaegi* for me to try. I put one *bundaegi* in my mouth and started chewing.

Min-Ho: So you ate the whole cup?

Anna: No, I could not even finish one little *bundaegi*. I had to spit it out and give the cup to my friend.

Min-Ho: Well, too bad. That food is a great source of protein.

Anna: I know, but I'd rather get my protein from a hamburger.

I produce silk for people. Isn't that enough? Then why do they eat our dead bodies? It's so cruel!

We always sing beautiful songs for people day and night! Then why do you want to eat us? If you keep eating us, we'll stop singing for you. Don't you know we are better than Mozart and Beethoven?

I don't know how people came to know I'm an excellent source of protein. I'm in danger of extinction!

UNIT 33 Future Foods

Futurologists say that fluctuating food prices and an increasing world population require us to rethink our food choices. The price of meat seems to rise continuously to the extent that, in another 5-7 years, the price of meat could double, turning it into a luxury item. In an article published by *BBC News*, food futurologist Morgaine Gaye says, "In the West, many of us have grown up with cheap, abundant meat. Rising prices mean we are now starting to see the return of meat as a luxury. As a result, we are looking for new ways to fill the meat gap." According to Gaye, one likely source of food in the future will be insects. According to researchers, insects are a great source of protein and provide as much nutritional value as traditional meats. Insects also are very cost-effective to raise, they consume less water than cattle, and raising them leaves a very small carbon footprint. In addition, there are some 1,400 species of insects that are edible.

How would humans consume insects? Would we have to pop an entire insect in our mouths like an hors d'oeuvre? Probably not, according to experts. Food producers would likely grind up crickets, grasshoppers, and other insects and reshape the meat so that it would look very much like traditional burgers and sausages.

The prospect of eating insects as a major food source is not as farfetched as you might think. A large part of the world's population already eats insects as a staple of their diet. In Africa, many people eat caterpillars and locusts; in Japan, wasps are considered a delicacy, and in Thailand, many people eat crickets. Western governments are researching the possibilities. The government of the Netherlands has invested one million Euros into research about the feasibility of insect farms. However, before insects can become a staple of the diet in North America and Europe, some method of overcoming people's traditional squeamishness toward insects will need to be found.

What do you think?

(1) Do you think that insects could become an important part of our diet in the near future?
(2) Have you ever eaten an insect? Would you be willing to try one?
(3) What is the most unusual type of food eaten in your country?
(4) What is the strangest thing that you personally have ever eaten?
(5) How often do you eat meat? What kind of meat do you prefer to eat?
(6) What is one food that you would never eat?
(7) Could you ever become a vegetarian or a vegan? Why or why not?

OPEN TO DEBATE 2

UNIT 34

Grade Inflation

Grace: Ji-Hoh, you look happy today. Did you receive some good news?

Ji-Hoh: Actually, I did. I just received some grade results, and I got an A+ in physics.

Grace: Wow! Congratulations! That's very impressive.

Ji-Hoh: Thanks. At my university, physics is one of the most difficult courses.

Grace: I can only imagine. I took physics in high school and was happy to get a B.

Ji-Hoh: Yeah, it's a very difficult subject, but I happen to enjoy math and science.

Grace: Is there any grade inflation at your university?

Ji-Hoh: I'm sure that there is for some majors but not in the physics major.

Grace: I believe you. I just don't think it's possible to make physics easy.

Ji-Hoh: Yeah, that's true. Now, if I can just get another A+ in English class.

Grace: Well, good luck with that.

What's wrong with grade inflation? It helps students get good jobs and eliminates complaints about tuition inflation among parents and students. Everybody is happy! Furthermore, according to economic theory, moderate inflation is better than deflation.

UNIT 34 — Grade Inflation

In late 2013, *The Harvard Crimson*, the university's student newspaper, published a statistic that showed what many observers had long suspected was true: grade inflation at the famous university was rampant. The newspaper stated that the median grade for undergraduates at Harvard was A-, and its most frequently awarded grade was A. However, grade inflation at Harvard and other great American universities is not new. According to anecdotal evidence, grade inflation started back in the 1960s at the height of the Vietnam War. If professors assigned low grades to students, those students might be forced out of college, drafted into the military, sent to Vietnam, and killed in war. Professors did not want to see this happen, so they began to assign higher grades.

According to some college administrators, grade inflation is due to the fact that current undergraduate students are more coddled and spoiled than any previous generation. Many students had "helicopter parents" who ensured that their children were never permitted to fail at anything or to be exposed to overly intense challenges. Children raised in such an environment grew up with an inflated sense of accomplishment, and they expect to receive high grades and continuing praise for all their academic achievements. Many employers echo these ideas. They say that recent college graduates expect "to be rewarded for showing up" to work, ask for a raise in salary after a month of average work, are unable to take criticism from their supervisor, and still expect their parents to intervene and help them.

Educators say that grade inflation deprives students of knowing their weakest and strongest areas. Grade inflation tells students that they do everything well. They fail to have the great educational experience of failing at something and learning how to recover. In the words of one Harvard professor, "Grade inflation represents a failure on the part of the faculty and its leadership to maintain academic standards."

What do you think?

(1) Are you shocked by the existence of grade inflation at Harvard?
(2) Is grade inflation a problem at the top universities in your country?
(3) Should universities restrict the percentages of A's, B's, and C's that professors can award?
(4) Were you ever given unfair grades in school? Were you ever given high grades that you didn't deserve?
(5) When you were in school, did you ever convince a professor to give you a higher grade?
(6) Do you know anyone who was a straight-A student throughout high school and college?
(7) Should political candidates be required to release a list of their college grades?

UNIT 35

Underpaid Actresses

Gun-Hoh: Hannah, I have a question about English, if you don't mind.

Hannah: Of course. What is your question?

Gun-Hoh: English speakers no longer use words like *fireman*, *salesman*, *policeman*, right?

Hannah: Yes, that's right. Those words are called "sexist" or "gender-biased" words.

Gun-Hoh: So, what words do you use in their place?

Hannah: We use "non-sexist" or "gender-neutral" words, such as *fire fighter*, *salesperson*, and *police officer*.

Gun-Hoh: But what about words like *actor/actress*?

Hannah: Well, nowadays, many English speakers use the word *actor* to refer to a male or female.

Gun-Hoh: Is it incorrect to use the word *actress* then?

Hannah: No, it's not wrong. It's just that the distinction is dying out, and the word *actor* will eventually be used for both sexes.

Gun-Hoh: I see. Thanks for your explanation.

What a stupid decision! How unfair!

Men: $30
Women: $27

Isn't it fair? Now we finally have real equality between men and women!

It's true that actresses are paid less than actors, and it seems that this trend will continue. So now the movie industry has decided to reduce the work of actresses by 10%. In addition, female moviegoers will pay 10% less than male moviegoers. No actresses have complained about their pay since the policy began.

UNIT 35 Underpaid Actresses

If you enjoy movies, you will certainly know the name Jennifer Lawrence. She starred in the *Hunger Games* films, and in 2015, with total earnings of $52 million, was the highest paid actress in the world. That figure sounds very impressive until you realize that the highest paid actor, Robert Downey, Jr., earned $80 million for the year. In the 2013 film *American Hustle*, the two female leads of the film, Jennifer Lawrence and Amy Adams, received a 7% cut of the film's profits, whereas the male stars of the film, Bradley Cooper, Christian Bale, and Jeremy Renner, all received a 9% cut. While Hollywood has long adored its great actresses and showered them with awards and adulation, the movie industry continues to underpay women in film and television, compared to their male counterparts. This reality is commonly referred to as the "gender pay gap."

The issue of the gender pay differential has received more media attention in recent years because more actresses are willing to speak out on the issue. Meryl Streep, whom many critics believe is the greatest contemporary actress, states that she still gets paid less than her male co-stars. Amanda Seyfried complains that, in many of her films, she received a tenth of what her male co-stars received on the same film. Gwyneth Paltrow expressed dismay when she found out about the huge pay gap between her and her *Iron Man* co-star, Robert Downey, Jr. However, in a rare victory for an actress, Scarlett Johansson earned the same amount as Chris Evans and Chris Hemsworth did in *Avengers: Age of Ultron* (2015).

The issue of pay disparity is not the only type of gender gap in Hollywood. A study of 2014 films showed that only 28.1% of the top 100 films for the year included significant female roles, and only 21% of the films had a female leading star. Also, women comprised only 1.9% of the directors, 11.2% of the writers, and 18.9% of the producers.

What do you think?

(1) Do you think Hollywood actresses have a legitimate complaint about the gender gap in salaries?
(2) Is there a similar pay gap between actors and actresses in your country?
(3) Do any of your favorite films have a female as the main star?
(4) Can you think of any popular TV shows that have an actress as the leading star?
(5) Have you ever met a famous actor/actress in person? Who was it?
(6) If your child wanted to become an actor/actress, how would you respond?
(7) The actress Reese Witherspoon said, "Women make up 50% of the population, so we should be receiving 50% of the roles on the screen." Do you agree with her?

OPEN TO **DEBATE 2**

OPEN TO DEBATE 2

UNIT 36

American Universities and Chinese Students

Su-Ji: Dylan, I have some great news!

Dylan: Really? What sort of news?

Su-Ji: I've been accepted at UCLA!

Dylan: Congratulations! That's great! When will you start?

Su-Ji: Next September. That's only six months away.

Dylan: Well, I'm happy for you. UCLA is a great school. What do you plan to major in?

Su-Ji: Economics. It's one of the top majors there, and I think it will help me get a good job when I return to Korea.

Dylan: Well, that sounds like a great choice, but please remember one thing.

Su-Ji: What's that?

Dylan: When you become a rich and famous CEO, just don't forget the little people who helped you along life's way, like your English teacher Dylan.

Su-Ji: Haha. Of course, I won't forget you.

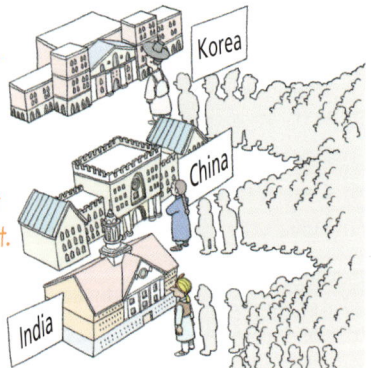

Korean people think education is the top priority. So it's natural that we send many students to the U.S.

China boasts the biggest population in the world. But the American people don't seem to know about it. We have to send many more students to prove it.

Our archrival, China, is sending a lot of students to the U.S. We have to send more students to catch up with them.

UNIT 36 — American Universities and Chinese Students

American universities are welcoming more and more international students. In fact, in the 2014-15 school year, the total international student enrollment at both public and private universities totaled 974,926. The top three places of origin of these international students were: China, 304,040 students (31.2%); India, 132,888 students (13.6%); and South Korea, 63,710 students (6.5%). As one might suspect, the two most populous countries in the world, China and India, sent the greatest numbers of students. However, China especially stands out in that its total number of students represents almost one-third of the entire body of international students.

Many universities in the United States are short on cash, so they are happy and willing to accept huge numbers of Chinese students. Over 60% of Chinese students pay for the full cost of their education at an American university. In effect, those payments subsidize the education of low-income American students. In addition, some universities profit further by charging additional fees for international students. These realities led one researcher to conclude that American universities are "addicted" to these wealthy Chinese students. According to academic sources, even the daughter of Chinese President Xi Jinping studied under an assumed name at Harvard.

Unfortunately, the huge influx of Chinese students has been fraught with problems. According to Zinch China, an educational consulting company, an overwhelming number of university applications by Chinese students are fraudulent. The company stated that as many as 90% of Chinese students submit fake recommendations, 70% have other people write their essays, 50% forge their high school transcripts, and 10% list academic awards and achievements that they did not receive. In 2015, federal prosecutors in the U.S. indicted 15 Chinese students for taking exams on behalf of others in order to obtain student visas. One consulting firm estimated that 3% of Chinese students end up being expelled from American universities due to poor academic performance or lack of academic integrity (i.e., cheating).

What do you think?

(1) Is the value of an American university education diminished by the acceptance of so many international students, seemingly for financial reasons?
(2) If you were an administrator at an American university, what steps would you take to correct the problems described above?
(3) Why are so many Chinese students studying abroad instead of staying in China?
(4) Are there many international students studying at universities in your country? What countries are they from?
(5) Have you ever considered studying abroad? Where would you like to study?
(6) Where would you prefer that your children attend college, at home or abroad?
(7) Have you ever submitted false or exaggerated information on an application for school or work?

OPEN TO DEBATE 2

UNIT 37

Cosmetics for Men?

Jessica: Min-Sung, you are looking great today! Have you had a makeover?

Min-Sung: What is a makeover?

Jessica: Well, it means that a person undergoes a complete course of cosmetic treatments to enhance their appearance.

Min-Sung: Oh, I see. No, I didn't have a makeover. I just had my hair styled, and I started to use some men's skincare products.

Jessica: Are you going on a big date?

Min-Sung: No, not at all. I'm a senior, and I think I will improve my chances of finding a good job if I look the best that I can.

Jessica: Well, that's a smart strategy. You're doing the right thing.

Min-Sung: Thanks. The job market is so competitive nowadays. I need every edge that I can get.

Jessica: Yeah, that's right. We may not like it, but employers often consider appearance strongly.

Min-Sung: Yes, that's so true.

— What are you doing?
— Can't you see I'm looking in the mirror?
— Now I finally believe some statistics that I saw recently.
— What are you talking about?
— They show that men spend more time looking in the mirror than women do.
— I agree. But there's a big difference.
— What do you mean?
— Women look in the mirror to put on makeup, and men look in the mirror to reflect on who they are.

UNIT 37   Cosmetics for Men?

In 2016, the size of the global market for men's cosmetics was estimated to be about $21.4 billion. It is clear that the market for men's makeup is booming. In a previous generation, men's toiletries consisted mostly of shampoo, deodorant, and shaving cream. But in the contemporary society, from London to New York to Seoul to São Paulo, men are buying facial cleansers, moisturizers, bronzers, concealers, anti-aging creams, and even mud masks. These are not women's products; they are specifically designed for men. More men are investing in products designed to make them look good. If they look good, they feel more attractive, more youthful, and more successful. The current trend was captured well by a makeup artist who said candidly, "I think men spend more time looking in the mirror than women do."

Nowhere is the upsurge in men's cosmetics more noticeable than in South Korea. According to Euromonitor, South Korean men spend more per capita on skincare than men in any other nation. The era of men's cosmetics in Korea began in 1997 with the Somang Cosmetics lotion "A Man with a Flower." It was furthered with the popularity of metrosexuals like Ahn Jung-hwan, who became famous for his role in the 2002 World Cup. Today, men's cosmetics represent 30% of cosmetics sales at Korean department stores.

The steadily increasing market for men's cosmetics has given rise to new companies seeking to capitalize on this market niche. In fact, it is not easy for companies that have traditionally specialized in women's cosmetics suddenly to break into the men's market. For example, the French firm L'Oréal and its subsidiaries, The Body Shop and Lancôme, are famous for their lines of women's cosmetics. Because of that association, the company's "Men Expert" line of men's cosmetics may not be readily accepted by men. Instead, smaller companies have entered the men's market with substantial success. Online vendors of men's cosmetics, such as Mënaji, 4Voo, and Kenmen, have reported substantial increases in sales.

What do you think?

(1) What is your opinion of the increasing sales of men's cosmetics? Is it a healthy trend?
(2) Why has Korea become so famous around the world for its cosmetics industry?
(3) Do you agree that "Men spend more time looking in the mirror than women do"?
(4) Do you know any businessmen who use cosmetics? Do you know any who refuse to use such cosmetics?
(5) Do you think that businessmen can actually improve their business by trying to "look good" with cosmetics?
(6) How much do you spend per month on cosmetics? What sort of products do you use most often?
(7) Koreans have not traditionally used deodorant. Why do you think that is true?

OPEN TO DEBATE 2

UNIT 38

The 40-Year-Old Virgin

Ashley: In-Su, I heard that you have a girlfriend now.

In-Su: Wow! News spreads quickly. Yes, it's true. I've been dating a girl named Ji-Young but only for about two months.

Ashley: I see. Well, you are in your late 20s now, right? You must be thinking about marriage.

In-Su: Well, I do think about marriage from time to time, but I need to save a lot of money before I take that serious step.

Ashley: It may not be possible to save enough to be completely financially secure.

In-Su: Yes, I know that, but I want to have enough money to buy our own apartment, have a car, and have some money in the bank.

Ashley: I see. Well, why not just live together before marriage?

In-Su: Oh, I could never do that! My parents would never approve of such an arrangement. Neither would Ji-Young's parents.

Ashley: Okay. I understand. I know a lot of people who have the same view.

We planned this group blind date to solve the 40-year-virgin problem. You have a great chance of success because you all have at least one thing in common: you're all virgins! So there's a good possibility that you can find your perfect match right here! Good luck! Start mingling!

UNIT 38 — The 40-Year-Old Virgin

The 40-Year-Old Virgin is a popular 2005 American romantic comedy film starring Steve Carell as the lead character, Andy Stitzer. Stitzer is a 40-year-old virgin who lives alone, plays video games, collects action figures, and spends time watching television with his elderly neighbors. Andy's co-workers invite him to join them in a poker game, and at that time, they learn that Andy is still a virgin. As a result of hearing this shocking news, the friends set about to help Andy lose his virginity. The friends give contradictory advice, creating numerous comedic situations. However, by the end of the film, Andy finally meets his match and marries a woman named Trish.

While it may seem funny that a man reaches the age of 40 and still has not slept with a woman, this topic is no laughing matter for many men in Japan. Take Takashi Sakai, for example. He is a healthy 41-year-old single man with a good job and an attractive smile. But he is one of an increasing number of Japanese men who are still virgins while reaching middle age. Sakai has never had a girlfriend, and he confesses that he has no idea about how he might find one. Another single male, a 49-year-old architect, stated that he had experienced romantic feelings for a woman only twice in his life. He was rebuffed by both women, leaving him emotionally devastated.

Surveys conducted in Japan in 2010 found that approximately one-fourth of single Japanese men in their 30s were still virgins. The researchers even coined a specific Japanese word, *yaramiso*, to describe them. The word was formed by combining *yarazu* (not to have sex) and *misoji* (a person in their 30s). The percentage of such virgins had increased by 3% from a similar survey conducted in 1992. During this period, Japan suffered a prolonged economic downturn, creating a tough and competitive financial situation. Many Japanese men began to feel as though they had lost their economic power.

What do you think?

(1) Does the phenomenon of the 40-year-old virgin exist in your country? How widespread is it?
(2) What social problems are created by the existence of a large percentage of single men?
(3) At what age do young men in your country usually get married? What about young women?
(4) Is marriage regarded as a necessity or a choice in your country?
(5) Nowadays, many young women choose a career over marriage. How are such women viewed in your country?
(6) Do most couples in your country wait until they get married before they sleep together?
(7) Oscar Wilde said, "Everything in the world is about sex, except sex. Sex is about power." What do you think he meant?

OPEN TO DEBATE 2

UNIT 39

Secret Lottery Winners?

Victoria: Mun-Hee, have you ever bought a lottery ticket?

Mun-Hee: Sure. I buy one occasionally but not too often.

Victoria: Have you ever won anything?

Mun-Hee: One time, I won 10,000 Korean won. I had a choice of taking the cash or getting more lottery tickets.

Victoria: What did you choose?

Mun-Hee: I chose the cash! I wanted the feeling of having a cash reward.

Victoria: That sounds like a good choice. What would you do if you won a huge lottery?

Mun-Hee: I would buy my parents a new house and car, treat myself to a round-the-world tour, and save the rest of the money.

Victoria: Oh, I'm really disappointed in your answer.

Mun-Hee: Why? I think those are good choices.

Victoria: Well, you didn't mention anything about helping your English teacher, Victoria.

Mun-Hee: Haha. Okay, I promise that, if I win a big lottery, I will treat you to a nice steak dinner.

"Wow! They know we're coming soon. We're generous enough to accept their suggestion, aren't we?"

No! I want all the money!

— Congratulations! You are the winner of the $100,000,000 lottery!
— Wow! This is so exciting! Thank you so much!
— Who are you going to share all this money with?
— Oh, we'll share it with our family, friends, and relatives, and then we'll donate the rest of it. However, before that, we'll have to share it with some people who are coming to our house for the money. We'll suggest to them that we can split the money 50-50 on the condition that they spare our lives.

UNIT 39 Secret Lottery Winners?

November 30, 2015, was a happy day for Craigory Burch Jr., a forklift operator who hit it big. On that day, Burch received a check from the Georgia Lottery in the amount of $434,272, his share of the winnings for successfully matching all five numbers in the November "Fantasy 5" lottery. He proudly held up an oversized version of his check for photographers, and his picture was published in local newspapers. Actually, he did not even have a choice about the publicity because, in the U.S. State of Georgia, all lottery winners must sign a form that states the following policies:

Pursuant to the Georgia Open Records Act, a prize winner's name, city, county, and state of residence and the amount of the prize won shall be regarded as matters of public record, which will be released by the Georgia Lottery Corporation (GLC). Accordingly, you will be asked to participate in interviews with GLC public relations personnel and media. This form acts as permission to use your name, photograph, quotes and likeness on the GLC website and in promotions of the GLC.

Only a few weeks later, Burch's good luck came to an end, when seven masked gunmen broke into his home. They aimed their guns directly at Burch, who was holding his 2-year-old child, and demanded money. Burch pleaded with the gunmen saying, "Don't do it, Bro! Don't do it in front of my kids! Please don't do it in front of my kids and girlfriend! I'll give you my bank card." Instead, the men shot and killed him. Within a few months, police arrested all seven perpetrators and charged them with malice murder, aggravated assault, armed robbery, home invasion, and possession of a firearm during the commission of a crime.

Burch's family members firmly believe that he was made a target because his lottery win was publicized. Most states, including Georgia, require lottery winners' names to be made public. Only a few states allow winners to remain anonymous.

What do you think?

(1) Should the Georgia Lottery have changed its policies about publicity after Burch was killed?
(2) Why do so many states require lottery winners' names to be made public?
(3) Are lottery winners' names made public in your country? Why or why not?
(4) Do you know anyone who won a large lottery? How did they handle their winnings?
(5) If you won a lottery, what steps would you take to protect your privacy?
(6) Have you ever won anything by playing the lottery? How much did you win?
(7) How much does a lottery ticket cost in your country? What is the largest prize that you have heard of?

OPEN TO DEBATE 2

UNIT 40

Male and Female: Attitudes toward Sex

Ye-Won: Angel, you've been living in Korea for two years now. Have you found a girlfriend?

Angel: No, not at all. Actually, I haven't been looking.

Ye-Won: Really? Don't you want to have a girlfriend?

Angel: Well, sure that would be great. However, I want to find love naturally, not by searching in desperation.

Ye-Won: Wow! You sound like a true romantic.

Angel: Well, I guess that I'm not the typical guy. I am not a playboy, like a lot of guys that I know.

Ye-Won: Well, that sounds good.

Angel: Yeah. I just want one woman to love and to spend the rest of my life in a loving relationship with her.

Ye-Won: Most women love your sort of attitude.

Angel: Thanks. I will just wait for the right woman to come my way.

Ye-Won: Good luck!

You must be kidding! Are you envious of their marriage?

— You have three wives? That's immoral!
— What're you talking about? We're in love and our polygamous marriage is happier than yours.
— It's against God's law!
— We don't think so. Love is love regardless of what kind of marriage we have.
— Then I have a question. Even though we have a monogamous marriage, we argue a lot. What's the secret of maintaining a harmonious marriage?
— We have no time to argue with each other because we're always busy loving each other.

UNIT 40 — Male and Female: Attitudes toward Sex

If you were a male student walking across the campus of Florida State University in 1982, you might have found yourself in a very unusual situation. An average-looking woman walks up to you and says something like this: "I've noticed you around campus, and I find you very attractive. Would you like to go to bed with me tonight?" If this happened to you, what would you have said? Here are some possibilities: (1) "Absolutely not! That would violate my own moral standards." (2) "I am flattered by your offer, but I'm in a committed relationship. No thanks." (3) "Yes, absolutely! Where shall we meet?"

As it turns out, this strange situation actually happened as part of a social experiment conducted by psychologists Russell Clark and Elaine Hatfield. The results of their now-famous study were published under the title "Gender Differences in Receptivity to Sexual Offers," in the *Journal of Psychology and Human Sexuality*, 1989. The research revealed that 75% of the male students who received the sexual proposition said "yes."

Later, the researchers conducted the experiment again, but this time, they enlisted an average-looking male actor to approach an attractive female student with the same type of proposition. Not one female student agreed to the man's offer. The result of the experiment showed that men and women responded as traditionalists expected them to. The researchers concluded by saying, "It may be that, as sociobiologists suggest, women are eager for love and commitment. Men are eager for sexual activity. Such theorizing is consistent with the data."

Another study asked both male and female college students how many sexual partners would they ideally like to have throughout their lifetime. The most common answer, given by both men and women, was one partner. However, the average of the men's answers totaled more than 60, but the average of the female's answers was a mere 2.7. The average of the answers was skewed by the fact that some respondents gave very high numbers.

What do you think?

(1) Are you shocked by the results of the study? What does it show about male and female attitudes?
(2) If this study were conducted on a college campus in your country, would the results be similar?
(3) Do you think male and female attitudes toward sex come from their biological nature or are they learned behaviors?
(4) In your society, is sex before marriage considered a moral failure? What about sex outside of marriage?
(5) Is human sexuality taught as an academic subject in university classes in your country?
(6) Do middle and high schools in your country educate young people about sex? Is the sex education program adequate?
(7) "The ideal situation is to have one sexual partner throughout your lifetime." Do you agree with that statement?

OPEN TO DEBATE 2

UNIT 41

Date Rape

Eun-Kyung: Taylor, I have some big news!

Taylor: Oh? Did you win the lottery?

Eun-Kyung: No, I got something a lot better than the lottery. I've been accepted at Duke University in the U.S.!

Taylor: Oh, wow! That's a great school. Congratulations! I'm happy for you.

Eun-Kyung: Thanks. But my parents are a little worried about safety issues.

Taylor: Well, most American campuses are safe. However, you do have to take precautions.

Eun-Kyung: What do you mean?

Taylor: Well, there are basic rules of safety that you should always follow.

Eun-Kyung: What kind of rules?

Taylor: I'm sure that a great university like Duke has seminars for all students about how to protect themselves against sexual harassment and date rape. Just check their website.

Eun-Kyung: Okay. I'll do that. Thanks for the tip.

What's the difference between them? Women seem to know the difference between yes and no while men don't. So universities plan to strengthen grammar classes for MALE students.

UNIT 41 — Date Rape

In the fall of 1990, Katie Koestner was a happy freshman at the College of William and Mary, the second oldest university in America, intending to study Japanese and chemistry. She didn't realize that she was about to experience a life-changing event. She had been dating a young man for less than two weeks. One evening, they enjoyed a romantic dinner at a French restaurant. She invited him back to her dorm room, where they danced and kissed. But then things began to change. He wanted to go further. She said "no." In fact, she said "no" more than ten times. However, the man would not listen, and he raped her.

Of course, Koestner went to the police, but in the end, the district attorney refused to prosecute the case because of a low chance of winning. It was a "he said, she said" type of case where a jury was unlikely to believe her account. In addition to the lack of prosecution, Koestner endured constant taunts from her classmates, who called her a liar. Some students vandalized her car and her dorm room. It would have been very easy for Koestner simply to give up in the face of all the opposition. However, she chose to become an advocate for victims of sexual assault. What happened to her captured national headlines and began a spirited debate. The words "date rape" and "no means no" became commonplace on college campuses.

On June 3, 1991, Koestner's face was on the cover of *Time* magazine, with the words "DATE RAPE" in big red letters. Later, her story was even turned into a film. Nowadays, Koestner serves as Executive Director of Take Back the Night Foundation, whose purpose is to combat sexual and domestic violence. Research shows that 1 in 3 women and 1 in 6 men worldwide experience some form of sexual violence. Less than 50% of victims report the crimes.

What do you think?

(1) Do you have a term for "date rape" in your language and country?
(2) How serious is the problem of date rape in your country?
(3) If a man is convicted of rape in your country, what sort of prison sentence does he receive? Is it a reasonable sentence in your opinion?
(4) Do you personally know anyone who has been a victim of sexual assault? What happened?
(5) Do universities in your country provide information to women about how to avoid being victims?
(6) Is it possible for a man to be the victim of sexual assault? In what ways?
(7) In Tokyo, there are subway cars that are for women only during certain hours. Does your country have a similar policy?

OPEN TO DEBATE 2

UNIT 42

Sexting

Ji-Won: Oh, David, you won't believe what happened to me!
David: What happened?
Ji-Won: This guy that I've been chatting with online asked me to send him explicit photos.
David: Oh, my! That's terrible! How did you meet this guy?
Ji-Won: Well, we were members of an online photography club, and we just exchanged messages about cameras and taking photographs.
David: Do you know where he's from?
Ji-Won: He said he lives in Australia, but I'm not sure that's true. He could live anywhere.
David: Well, I think that you should report him to the photography club administrator and also block him from contacting you again.
Ji-Won: Actually, I've already done that, but I don't think there's anything else that I can do.
David: I guess not, since you don't know where he lives. Please be very careful when you're online.
Ji-Won: Oh, I've learned my lesson. I'm no longer a member of that photography club, and I won't be joining any other online clubs.

What did I do wrong? I just got undressed because it was too hot! Then I wanted to see nude pictures of myself to see if my exercise program was having a good effect.

Let me go! I have a right to dress as I please and to take pictures of myself as I please!

I'm a smart phone. I'm so smart that everybody loves me. But when you abuse me by sending explicit pictures of yourself to others, it makes me very angry. You're going to pay a heavy price for your abuse!

UNIT 42 Sexting

In 2012, a new word made its way into *Merriam-Webster's Collegiate Dictionary* for the first time. That was the word sexting, which was formed by combining the words *sex* and *texting*. As you can probably guess, the word sexting refers to sending and receiving sexually explicit messages and images, usually between cell phones. The Pew Research Center has determined that there are three types of messages that can be classified as sexting. These are exchanges of messages and images (1) between two romantic partners that are kept private between the two of them; (2) between partners but that are shared with others; and (3) between people who are not yet in a romantic relationship, but where at least one person hopes to be.

According to the website DoSomething.org, the practice of sexting is widespread. Anyone who is tempted to engage in sexting should remember the following important facts:

- 17% of sexters share the messages they receive with others, and 55% of those share them with more than one person.
- 61% of all sexters who have sent nude images admit that they were pressured to do it at least once.
- 22% of teen girls have reported sending nude or semi-nude images, while only 18% of teen boys have.
- Sending or receiving a sexually suggestive text or image under the age of 18 is considered child pornography and can result in criminal charges.
- 24% of high-school age teens (ages 14 to 17) and 33% of college-age students have been involved in a form of nude sexting.
- 11% of teen girls ages 13 to 16 have been involved with sending or receiving sexually explicit messages.

Why would a teenage girl participate in sexting? Research shows that 40% do it as a joke, 34% do it to feel sexy, and 12% do it because they feel pressured to do it.

What do you think?

(1) Does sexting exist in your country? How widespread is it?
(2) What harm can come from sexting? Can it lead to other more dangerous behaviors?
(3) Have any organizations in your country issued warnings about the dangers of sexting?
(4) Have you read about anyone who was a perpetrator or a victim of sexting? What happened?
(5) Do high schools in your country have any policies about sexting? What are the policies?
(6) What sort of punishment should someone face for sexting pictures of those who are under age 18?
(7) Do you think it's okay for adult romantic partners to practice private sexting? Why or why not?

OPEN TO DEBATE 2

UNIT 43

Cheating Students

Jung-Hwa: Lauren, I have a problem. I need your advice.

Lauren: Sure. What sort of problem do you have?

Jung-Hwa: My best friend wants me to help him cheat on an exam. I don't know what to do.

Lauren: Oh my! That's terrible. What did he ask you to do?

Jung-Hwa: Well, I take very good notes in class, and I organize them better than most students.

Lauren: Okay. That's good.

Jung-Hwa: My friend wants a copy of all my notes to study for the final exam.

Lauren: Hmmm.... I'm not sure that would actually be classified as cheating. He would still have to learn the material.

Jung-Hwa: Well, I thought it might not be a good thing to do.

Lauren: I think you should ask your teacher if that would be cheating. Maybe she will say it's okay to share your notes.

Jung-Hwa: Okay. That's a good idea. Thanks.

Cheating is so rampant on the university campus that the Harvard faculty has decided that they'll no longer give exams and assignments in order to get rid of cheating. Instead, they will judge students' scholastic performance by how fast they surf the Internet because all knowledge is available online.

Solar-powered mouse: It boasts lightning speed, and no battery is needed. But if it's not sunny, it quickly becomes nonfunctional.

Nuclear-powered mouse: It goes thousands of years with no power failure, whether or not it's sunny.

I was an all-A student. But the university's new policy has made me drop out of school because I can't afford to buy a speedy mouse. I am a victim of today's nonsense!

UNIT 43 Cheating Students

In May 2012, a teaching assistant at Harvard University began to correct the final take-home exams for a class entitled "Government 1310: Introduction to Congress." He noticed that there were many similarities among students' answers, similarities that could have only come from cheating. The professor of the class conducted an investigation that indicated that approximately 125 students, about half of the class, had cheated on the exam. Eventually, after the investigation of each individual student's exam was completed, 70 students were forced to withdraw from the university.

If cheating is happening at Harvard, it's probably happening everywhere. In fact, studies show that about 75% of college students admit to cheating. With so many students cheating, it is a safe conclusion that cheating is an acceptable practice among students. However, it's not a new practice. According to the *Boston Globe*, the percentage of students who admit to cheating has remained constant since the first surveys were conducted in 1963. While the Internet may have introduced new methods of cheating, the number of cheating students has remained the same. It's very clear that whatever measures that have been introduced in the last 50 years to stop cheating have not worked.

Why do students cheat? A blog post on GlobalPost.com offers some explanations. First, there may be ambiguous attitudes among students about what actually constitutes cheating. For example, some students may think that simply paraphrasing an author's work is not plagiarism. Second, competitive pressures on contemporary students are immense. Students may sacrifice integrity for success. Third, students' lack of respect toward their university may lead them to think that the university does not deserve high standards. Fourth, many students may not have even read the university rules about cheating, so they may cheat by accident. Finally, students are motivated by self-interest. They may think that cheating contributes to a better return on their investment of time and finances.

What do you think?

(1) Are you shocked to hear that cheating took place at Harvard?
(2) Do you think the punishment of being expelled from the university was reasonable?
(3) Can you estimate the percentage of cheating students at the top universities in your country?
(4) Do you know anyone who was caught cheating in high school or college? What happened?
(5) If your best friend asked you to help him cheat on a test, would you help?
(6) If your romantic partner asked you to help them cheat, would you do it?
(7) Did you ever cheat on an exam in high school or college? What happened?

OPEN TO DEBATE 2

UNIT 44

Nonstop Hacking

Ryan: You won't believe what happened to me!

Ji-Su: I can't imagine. What happened?

Ryan: I received a phone call from my bank that my credit card account was hacked.

Ji-Su: Oh, that's terrible! How did they know?

Ryan: The bank said that someone from Nigeria tried to get a cash advance on my credit card.

Ji-Su: Well, it's obvious that you aren't in Nigeria.

Ryan: Right! The bank has sophisticated software that recognized the suspicious nature of the transaction.

Ji-Su: Well, at least they caught the problem before anything bad happened.

Ryan: Yeah, that's good, but now I have to change all of my credit cards and bank information.

Ji-Su: That's too bad, but you can be thankful because it could have been a lot worse.

– We have finally developed a system that no hacker can break into.
– Don't you know I'm a computer genius? No system is safe from my hacking. My hacking skills will always outperform your security measures.
– I know it's a game of cat and mouse. May I make a suggestion?
– Yes, of course.
– Protecting our system costs a lot of money. We're willing to pay you regularly on the condition that you don't hack our system.
– Good idea! Then everybody wins!

UNIT 44 Nonstop Hacking

One would think that, if any country would have secure websites, that country would be the United States. After all, the Internet was created in the U.S. and was based on an early system of computer communication designed for military purposes. Yet in recent years, numerous American government websites have been among those that have been successfully hacked. Hacked American websites include the U.S. State Department, the Central Intelligence Agency, the White House, the U.S. Senate, the U.S. Postal Service, the National Oceanic and Atmospheric Administration, the U.S. Investigations Services, and the Office of Personnel Management. In 2011, even the Pentagon, the headquarters of the U.S. military, was broken into by foreign hackers who stole 24,000 files. In early 2015, the Twitter and Youtube sites of the American military's central command were hacked by supporters of the Islamic State. After taking control of the sites, the hackers posted threatening messages and videos. In response, the American military stated that military networks were not compromised, and the social media sites were restored after a short period. According to the U.S. military's cyber command, about 250,000 potential hackers browse the Pentagon's computer defenses every hour.

In late 2015, U.S. military officials were aghast when China showcased a new stealth fighter for sale at the Dubai Air Show. The fighter, called a Shenyang FC-31, is a virtual copy of the U.S. F-35 joint strike fighter, leaving the Americans with the conclusion that China had stolen top secret designs. In mid-2016, the South Korean National Police Agency revealed that more than 40,000 documents related to the defense industry were stolen, apparently by North Korean hackers. The successful hack enabled North Korea to obtain wing designs for an American F-15 jet fighter and for parts of spy planes.

If the U.S. military and government can be hacked, is it possible for any individual to achieve security of their own files?

What do you think?

(1) Why isn't the American military able to secure its own websites?
(2) Have you read about any serious examples of hacking in your country? What happened?
(3) Do you think the government's data files about you are secure?
(4) Has your computer or personal information ever been hacked? What did you do?
(5) Has a stranger ever called you asking for personal information? How did you respond?
(6) Are you familiar with ransomware? Do you know anyone who has been a victim of it?
(7) What sort of virus protection do you use on your computer? How effective is it?

OPEN TO DEBATE 2

UNIT 45

Preserving the Rain Forest

Ji-Yung: James, I heard you mention the term "reverse culture shock." Could you explain what that means?

James: Sure. Reverse culture shock occurs when someone has lived in another country for a while and then returns to his home country.

Ji-Yung: And you are shocked by your own culture?

James: Yes. Take me, for example. I'm an American, but I've lived in Korea for a long time.

Ji-Yung: So when you return to the U.S., you feel some shock?

James: Yes, I do. Here's a good example. Since I've lived in Korea, I've become a very good recycler.

Ji-Yung: What do you mean?

James: When I go to a hamburger restaurant here in Korea, I always recycle my drink cup and straw, for example.

Ji-Yung: Americans don't do that?

James: No, not at all. The last time I went to a fast-food restaurant in the U.S., the restaurant provided no method to recycle my huge plastic cup. I had to throw it in the trash.

Ji-Yung: That's terrible! Restaurants should be forced to recycle that type of item.

James: I agree with you, and that's how I experienced reverse culture shock.

People have cut down all the trees in the world except for three trees.

I'm dying because of the lack of oxygen. Humans have destroyed every forest, and I am about to become extinct because of their brutality.

I don't have time to care about you! I have to cut down all the trees left and buy more oxygen ASAP. I'm running out of oxygen.

UNIT 45 Preserving the Rain Forest

Studies show that the world's rain forests are disappearing at the rate of 6,000 acres every hour. That is an area of about 4,000 football fields. Almost 90% of West Africa's rain forests have been destroyed. Since humans arrived in Madagascar, almost two-thirds of its original rain forest has been eradicated. If the present rate of deforestation continues, the tropical rain forests in Indonesia will be logged out in ten years and those in Papua New Guinea in 13-16 years. Brazil has declared deforestation of the Amazon as a national emergency. Experts say that 60% of the Amazon rain forest could be wiped out by 2030.

More than half of the world's species of plants and animals live in the rain forest. When rain forests are cut down, not only are the plants destroyed, but the animals that live in those forests have to move. According to some biologists, as much as one-fourth of all species on Earth could be exterminated within 50 years because of the removal of native habitats. Plants and animals are not the only living things to be at risk. Human beings need oxygen to breathe, and the rainforests produce oxygen and clean the atmosphere. The eradication of rain forests disrupts the earth's ecosystem, climate, and water cycle.

People are concerned about the destruction of the rain forests but may feel confused as to what they can do about the problem. Average citizens can vote for politicians who support the preservation of the rain forests. Governments should not allow timber-harvesting companies to "clear cut" large areas of forests. Those companies should be required to plant new trees whenever they cut down old trees. One practical step that people can take is to refuse to buy animals as pets, such as parrots and iguanas, which are often imported illegally. Also, people can choose to purchase items that are Rainforest Alliance Certified™ products. Finally, of course, we can all recycle and reuse items whenever possible.

What do you think?

(1) Are you personally concerned about the destruction of the world's rain forests? Why or why not?
(2) Does your country have any forests? Are they being preserved?
(3) Is natural wood used very much as a construction material in your country?
(4) Would you consider having a rare type of pet, such as an endangered species? Why or why not?
(5) Would you ever like to be an ecotourist (visiting a natural area of the world)? Where would you go?
(6) Do you take public transportation as a means of protecting the environment? Why or why not?
(7) Do you consider yourself a good recycler? What sorts of items do you recycle?

OPEN TO DEBATE 2

UNIT 46

Drug Cartels

Se-Joon: Julia, you are from Australia, right?

Julia: Yes, I am. Why do you ask?

Se-Joon: Did you read the story about the Australians who were executed in Indonesia for drug trafficking?

Julia: Oh, I think you are referring to Andrew Chan and Myuran Sukumaran. Yes, I think every Australian was aware of their sad plight.

Se-Joon: What was your opinion of their execution?

Julia: Well, they were convicted of heroin smuggling, which is a serious crime. However, I am opposed to the death penalty.

Se-Joon: Yeah, I agree with you. I could understand a period of imprisonment, but putting them to death seems too severe.

Julia: Yes, it was sad. For that reason, I don't think I'll ever travel to Indonesia.

Se-Joon: Well, you are not a drug trafficker, so you don't have anything to worry about.

Julia: True, but you never know when someone might slip some drugs into your suitcase.

Se-Joon: Okay. I see your point.

I agree. Something must be done for our survival!

Good idea! Go ahead! If there is only one drug dealer left, we can easily cope with him.

I'm worried about the bottom line and the increasing competition among the cartels!

Let's have a gunfight and let the winner monopolize the drug market! That's a fair solution, isn't it?

UNIT 46 Drug Cartels

The word "cartel" refers to an international syndicate of producers of a product who agree together to regulate prices and production. The word is often used of criminal organizations that maintain a distribution system for illegal drugs. When most people hear the term "drug cartel," they think of Mexico, Columbia, and the United States. However, drug cartels actually exist in all areas of the world. Even Asia has its own drug cartels. China has many branches of transnational crime organizations, called triads, that include such groups as the 14K, Sun Yee On, and Shui Fong. Japan also has similar organizations, including Kyushu Seido-kai, Sumiyoshi-kai, and Yamaguchi-gumi.

In the 1990s, after the demise of the drug cartels in Cali and Medellín, Columbia, the influence of Mexican drug cartels increased dramatically. By 2007, the Mexican cartels controlled 90% of the cocaine entering the U.S. The arrests of some key leaders of the drug cartels in Mexico led to a dramatic increase in drug violence as the remaining cartels fought for control of the trafficking routes into the U.S. Analysts estimate that wholesale earnings from the Mexican cartels' illicit drug sales range from $14 to $49 billion annually. By 2013, the death toll of the Mexican Drug War was estimated at more than 120,000, not including another 27,000 who are missing.

The level of punishment for individuals who sell drugs and buy drugs varies greatly around the world. In the U.S., statistics show that all drug offenders face many years in prison, and African-Americans are imprisoned at a much higher rate than others. In Malaysia and Thailand, those who sell drugs can be punished with death. Likewise, in China, some drug crimes result in execution. In Vietnam, if you are arrested with more than 1.3 pounds of heroin, you face automatic execution. Selling drugs in Saudi Arabia almost always results in the death penalty.

What do you think?

(1) Are there any drug cartels in your country? Do you know of any way to buy illegal drugs?
(2) What is the punishment for selling drugs in your country? What about for using drugs?
(3) Do you support applying the death penalty to drug traffickers?
(4) Even if you are not a drug user, would you have some fear of traveling to a country with very strict penalties for drug users?
(5) Do you consider alcohol, coffee, tea, and carbonated drinks to be drugs?
(6) If you saw a drug deal taking place on a street corner, what would you do?
(7) If your best friend were using drugs, would you report him to the police? What if he were selling drugs?

OPEN TO DEBATE 2

UNIT 47

Euthanasia

Olivia: Dong-Min, did you read about that case of euthanasia in Korea?

Dong-Min: Yes, I did. It was about a woman who was in a coma for 459 days.

Olivia: Yes, that's right, and the Supreme Court of Korea granted her the right to die.

Dong-Min: Well, it was the first case of legalized euthanasia in Korea, so that was a big step for Korea.

Olivia: Do you have the concept of a "living will" in Korea?

Dong-Min: What exactly is a living will?

Olivia: It's a document that states that, if I become terminally ill, I do not want to be kept alive artificially with machines.

Dong-Min: Oh, I've heard about that, but I don't think we have it in Korea.

Olivia: That's too bad. Without this type of legal avenue, the Supreme Court will have to decide each individual case.

Dong-Min: That would become very cumbersome and unfeasible.

Olivia: I agree. I think that Korea needs to recognize the legality of a living will.

Dong-Min: Yeah, it's a good idea, but it could take some time before it becomes legal.

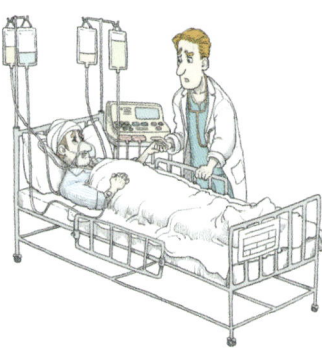

— I have severe pains all over!
— Don't worry. We'll take care of you.
— I want to be euthanized!
— No way! It's illegal here.
— Then how can I foot the bill? I'm broke!
— You're broke?
— Yes, absolutely!
— Then we have a way to save on your medical bills.
— What do you mean?
— From now on, we'll prescribe only aspirin, and then you'll pass away in a couple of days.

UNIT 47 Euthanasia

Euthanasia refers to the practice of intentionally ending a life in order to relieve pain and suffering, which could be physical or emotional. In 2001, the Netherlands became the first country in the world to legalize euthanasia and assisted suicide. Supporters of the law argued that it would help physicians end pain and suffering for their patients in a compassionate manner. Opponents of the law argued that it would allow the taking of human life under questionable circumstances and that it would be a "slippery slope" leading to unintended consequences, such as healthy people taking their lives. Dr. Theo Boer, Professor of Ethics at the Protestant Theological University at Groningen, was an early proponent of the new law. In 2007, he wrote, "There doesn't need to be a slippery slope when it comes to euthanasia. A good euthanasia law, in combination with the euthanasia review procedure, provides the safeguards for a stable and relatively low number of euthanasia patients." Many physicians and ethicists agreed with Boer.

In 2014, however, Boer expressed regret about embracing the euthanasia law. He wrote, "We were wrong—terribly wrong, in fact." Boer observed that the number of euthanasia deaths in the Netherlands had continually increased. From 2008 to 2013, the number of reported euthanasia deaths increased from 2,331 to 4,829. Also, when the law was first enacted, it was assumed that the decision for euthanasia would rest upon a strong doctor-patient relationship. However, as the years passed, organizations such as the "End of Life Clinic" were established, along with a network of what Boer called "travelling euthanizing doctors." Many of these doctors would see a patient only three times before administering a lethal injection. Also, some Dutch pediatricians wanted to extend euthanasia to children under 12. Finally, questionable decisions were made in cases of euthanasia, such as the case of one clinic that ended a woman's life simply because she didn't want to live in a nursing home.

What do you think?

(1) Is euthanasia legal in your country? Do you think it should be?
(2) Under what circumstances should euthanasia be allowed?
(3) Have you heard about anyone who was in a coma for a long time? What happened?
(4) If you knew that your baby growing in the womb was deformed, would you choose to abort it?
(5) If you were severely injured and in a coma for a long time, would you want the life support machines unplugged?
(6) If it were possible to know the day of your death, would you want to know?
(7) If you could choose the way that you would die, what method would you choose?

OPEN TO DEBATE 2

UNIT 48

Israel versus Palestine

Joshua: Eun-Ji, I'm going to be away for a couple of weeks.
Eun-Ji: Oh? Where are you going?
Joshua: I'm going to visit Israel. It's my first time, so I'm very excited about it.
Eun-Ji: Wow! May I ask: Are you Jewish?
Joshua: No, I'm not Jewish. I'm a Christian, and I want to visit some of the famous sites mentioned in the Bible.
Eun-Ji: Oh, I see. Are you going alone?
Joshua: No, I'm going with a group from my church.
Eun-Ji: Oh that's good, but don't you think it's dangerous? I just saw on the news where there were some stabbings in Israel.
Joshua: Well, there is violence there from time to time, but I will be a tourist, so I think I will be safe.
Eun-Ji: Okay. Just be careful. Which sites are you most interested in seeing?
Joshua: I think I'd like to visit the Sea of Galilee. That's where much of Jesus' ministry took place.
Eun-Ji: Well, it should be a wonderful trip. Take lots of pictures, so I can see them when you return.
Joshua: Of course.

The purpose of this declaration of war on Earth is to provide a chance for Israel and Palestine to make a peace treaty. Just pretend to attack them!

— Oh my! The extraterrestrials are invading us!
— It's true! Let's band together to defeat them. We can live to fight each other another day.
— I agree. But don't forget we're archrivals! As soon as we prevail over them, we'll need to resume our war immediately!
— Ha, ha! We're on the same page!

UNIT 48 — Israel versus Palestine

In the 1996 epic science fiction film *Independence Day*, the entire world is attacked by an alien race bent on destroying Planet Earth. By the end of the film, all the inhabitants of Earth have united against the invaders. As part of this newfound unity, even Israelis and Palestinians are shown embracing. Unfortunately, real life is different, and the Israeli-Palestinian conflict continues to be known as the world's "most intractable conflict." While Israel has managed to reconcile with Egypt and Jordan, Israel has failed to reach a lasting peace agreement with Palestine. The most important issues are: mutual recognition, demarcation of borders, provisions for security, establishment of water rights, control of Jerusalem, Israeli settlements in Palestine, Palestinian freedom of movement, and the Palestinian right of return to Israel.

The violence that has been spawned by this seemingly unsolvable conflict is seen on a regular basis on news reports around the world. Numerous attempts have been made to broker a solution that would allow both groups of people to live in harmony. The preferred solution is usually called the "two-state solution," meaning that an independent Palestinian state would exist alongside the State of Israel, as established in 1948. Polls taken in 2007 showed that a majority of both Israelis and Palestinians preferred the two-state solution above all other ideas. Indeed, most Israelis believe that the Palestinians' demand for an independent state is reasonable. However, mutual distrust and disagreements about the implementation of any peaceful co-existence remain unabated. Both sides are extremely skeptical that the other side would uphold obligations in an agreement.

Potential solutions to the conflict were made even more elusive when the Palestinian Authority split into the factions of Fatah and Hamas in 2007. After Hamas took over the Gaza Strip, all relations between Israel and Palestine were cancelled, except for limited humanitarian efforts. However, a Palestinian Unity Government, composed of both Fatah and Hamas, was formed in 2014. In spite of that unified front, no peace agreement has been achieved.

What do you think?

(1) Have you ever studied about the Israeli-Palestinian conflict? Do you have a good understanding of it?
(2) If you could act as a peace broker between the two groups, what solutions would you offer?
(3) What share of blame should be placed on the United Nations for this continuing conflict?
(4) Have you ever met a person from Israel or from Palestine? What was your impression?
(5) Do you believe that Israel and Palestine will achieve a peace agreement in your lifetime?
(6) Do you have any desire to visit Israel as a tourist? Why or why not?
(7) If you had a chance to visit Palestine, would you go? Why or why not?

OPEN TO DEBATE 2

UNIT 49

Democrats and Republicans

Sung-Min: Morgan, you're American, right?

Morgan: Yes, I am. Why do you ask?

Sung-Min: Well, I'm interested in American politics. I was just wondering if you can vote even though you live and work in Korea.

Morgan: Yes, of course, I can vote by what's called an "absentee ballot."

Sung-Min: Oh? Your local voting office sends you a ballot by mail?

Morgan: Yes, they do, and I always vote in the presidential election.

Sung-Min: Are you from a red state or a blue state?

Morgan: Neither. I am from Florida, which is a swing state. It sometimes votes Republican and sometimes Democratic.

Sung-Min: If you don't mind me asking, who do you plan to vote for in the upcoming election?

Morgan: I don't mind you asking, if you don't mind me not answering. It's top secret!

Sung-Min: Haha. Okay. I see. Well good luck to your candidate.

I don't want to be a referee in this dirty game! Neither of them is observing the rules

Everybody knows you lied about your emails. You are not qualified to be the President of the United States.

A liar is better than a womanizer! You're just a dirty grandpa! Drop out of the race immediately! You can always spend your time chasing skirts!

UNIT 49 — Democrats and Republicans

International observers of American politics are often confused about the differences between the two major political parties in the United States: the Democrats and the Republicans. Unless one studies the American political system and its parties thoroughly, it may be difficult to see exactly what the distinctions are. The history of the Republican Party begins with Abraham Lincoln, who served from 1861 to 1865. The party is currently identified with what is known as *American conservatism*. It supports free market capitalism, free enterprise, a strong business climate with limited regulation, a strong national defense, a limited size of government, restrictions on labor unions, opposition to abortion and same-sex marriage, and upholding of traditional moral values.

The Democratic Party was founded around 1828, making it the oldest active political party in the world. Its contemporary political viewpoint is known as *modern liberalism*. It promotes socially liberal ideals, including a strong dedication to social justice. Democrats typically support economic equality, welfare provisions for the poor and disadvantaged, labor unions, universal health care, equal opportunity, strong consumer protection, and strong environmental protection. If a voter is neither a Republican nor Democrat, they are an independent or a member of a minor political party, such as the Libertarian Party or Green Party.

The American presidential election is held in November every four years. The U.S. follows an 18th century electoral system in which the most important weight is placed on how individual states vote and not on the total popular vote nationwide. As a result, in recent years, some states are known as "red states" because they always vote Republican, and some states are known as "blue states" because they always vote Democratic. That leaves about 11 states that are called "purple states" or "swing states." The most important swing states are Ohio, Florida, and Pennsylvania. The presidential candidate who wins two of those states is likely to become president.

What do you think?

(1) Are you interested in American politics? How do you stay informed about it?
(2) If you had to choose an American political party, would you be a Republican, Democrat, or independent?
(3) How many Republican presidents can you name? How many Democratic presidents?
(4) Does your country have political parties similar to the Republicans and Democrats?
(5) Some people think that all politicians are dishonest. Do you agree or disagree?
(6) Do you always vote for president in your country? Why or why not?
(7) Which American politician do you view favorably? Which do you view negatively?

OPEN TO DEBATE 2

UNIT 50

Racial Equality in the U.S.

Sa-Rah: Nathan, do you think the U.S. has achieved racial equality?

Nathan: Well, certainly, we've made some progress. However, I think that we still have a long way to go.

Sa-Rah: Really? But you elected an African-American president and then re-elected him. Doesn't that show progress?

Nathan: Yes, of course, that's a step in the right direction. However, 60% of blacks say that job discrimination against them continues.

Sa-Rah: Oh, that's not good.

Nathan: Yes, and many blacks are distrustful of the police.

Sa-Rah: That's terrible!

Nathan: Unfortunately, blacks are six times more likely to be imprisoned than whites, and Hispanics are three times more likely.

Sa-Rah: Wow! Those are shocking statistics.

Nathan: They are, and that's why I say that, while Americans have made progress, they need to do a lot more.

Sa-Rah: Okay. I see what you mean.

— You went through a red light. I'm going to write you a ticket!
— The man behind me broke the same law. Why aren't you giving him a ticket?
— I'll get to him later.
— Why am I alone getting a ticket? Is it because I'm black?
— Well, you are more noticeable.
— This is not fair!
— Why don't you paint yourself white whenever you drive? It will help!

UNIT 50 — Racial Equality in the U.S.

The defining moment of the American Civil Rights Movement took place on August 28, 1963, when Dr. Martin Luther King, Jr., delivered his famous "I Have a Dream" speech in Washington, DC. In fact, a group of scholars ranked this address as the top American speech of the 20th century. In the speech, Dr. King called for an end to racism in the United States and for civil and economic rights for all people, including African-Americans. He dreamed of a day when his children would "not be judged by the color of their skin but by the content of their character."

Some would say King's dream has been achieved. In 2008, the United States elected its first African-American president, Barack Obama. One of the richest women in the entire country is a black woman, Oprah Winfrey. Thus, many would say that African-Americans have achieved full equality. However, a poll taken by Pew Research in mid-2016 showed that whites and blacks in America view the issues of race and equality very differently. When Americans were asked if race relations in the U.S. were "generally bad" or "generally good," 61% of blacks and 58% of Hispanics chose "generally bad," while only 45% of whites chose that evaluation. When asked if the country had made enough changes to achieve racial equality, 38% of whites said yes, but 88% of blacks and 70% of Hispanics said that more changes were needed. Indeed, 43% of blacks expressed doubt that the country would ever make the changes that would lead to equal rights for black people.

Are blacks treated less fairly than whites in the workplace? A total of 64% of blacks say yes, but only 22% of whites agree. By overwhelming numbers, blacks also say that they have experienced unfair treatment. Some 47% of blacks state that other people were suspicious of them, and about 45% say that people around them acted as though they weren't smart. Only 10% of whites report such unfair treatment.

What do you think?

(1) Are you surprised that such a large number of African-Americans believe equality has still not been realized?
(2) What was your reaction when you heard that the U.S. had elected its first black president?
(3) Who are the major groups of minorities in your country? Do they suffer from any discrimination?
(4) Are there any minorities who are in positions of power in your country? Who are they?
(5) Would you like to see more immigrants come to your country? Why or why not?
(6) Does your country have any Chinatowns? How big are they? Do you ever visit the area?
(7) Do you have any friends who are members of a minority group?

UNIT 51

Artificial Intelligence

Sophia: Jae-Hyeon, you'll never guess what I did today.

Jae-Hyeon: I have no idea. What did you do?

Sophia: I joined eharmony.com! I'm going to find the perfect boyfriend.

Jae-Hyeon: Oh, I've heard of that website. They claim that their software can find the best match for you.

Sophia: Yes, it's called the Compatibility Matching System®, and it finds a good romantic match.

Jae-Hyeon: Well, I'm not so sure about this. Wouldn't you rather make your own choice?

Sophia: Actually, I've been trying that my whole life, and I still haven't found the right one.

Jae-Hyeon: Okay. I see what you mean, but you can still reject the computer's suggestions, right?

Sophia: Of course, but I think that it's usually successful.

Jae-Hyeon: What makes you say that?

Sophia: The website claims that 438 couples who met through the site get married every day.

Jae-Hyeon: That sounds impressive, but I'll stick with the old-fashioned way.

Artificial intelligence has now beaten humans at both chess and *baduk*, so I'm the last hope of mankind! I have to win in order to prove that human beings are still better than robots!

No way! Humans will have to kneel down before us creatures of artificial intelligence. We know all your weaknesses too well! You have created a MONSTER!

UNIT 51 Artificial Intelligence

Who is smarter: man or computer? One answer to that question can be found in the human-machine matchups of intelligence that have taken place in recent years. In 1996, IBM developed a chess-playing computer called Deep Blue, which was then scheduled for a six-game match against the reigning world chess champion, Garry Kasparov. Deep Blue won the first game of the match, but Kasparov won three and tied two of the following five games, meaning that Kasparov defeated Deep Blue by a score of 4-2. A rematch was scheduled for the following year, and Deep Blue was heavily upgraded. In May 1997, Deep Blue won the six-game rematch 3½-2½ and became the first computer system to defeat a reigning world champion in a match under the standard rules of chess tournaments. Kasparov accused IBM of cheating and demanded a rematch. IBM refused and dismantled Deep Blue.

In 2011, another notable matchup of man and machine took place on the popular American TV game show *Jeopardy*. Success on the show requires a massive knowledge of general facts, and IBM designed a supercomputer called Watson, which they crammed with four terabytes of content, including the full text of Wikipedia. Watson was pitted against the two greatest Jeopardy champions, Ken Jennings and Brad Rutter. In the end, Watson trounced his two human opponents, racking up $77,147 in winnings, compared to $24,000 for Jennings and $21,600 for Rutter.

Yet another match between man and machine took place in Korea in March 2016, when Lee Sedol, a Korean master of *baduk*, played a five-game match against a computer program known as AlphaGo. The computer program won the series 4-1. Google DeepMind, the developer of AlphaGo, won the $1 million prize but stated that the winnings would be donated to charities. Lee received $170,000 ($150,000 for participation in the tournament and $20,000 for winning one game). After the game, the Korea Baduk Association awarded AlphaGo the highest Go grandmaster rank, an "Honorary 9 Dan."

What do you think?

(1) Do these human-computer matchups prove that computers are smarter than humans?
(2) What lessons can we humans learn from these examples of the triumph of artificial intelligence?
(3) Have you ever used artificial intelligence to help you accomplish a task? What happened?
(4) Do you believe that you will own a robot in your lifetime?
(5) Can computers make more rational decisions than human beings?
(6) Can computers be used to make moral decisions?
(7) Do you think that computers can make better romantic matchups than humans?

OPEN TO DEBATE 2

UNIT 52

An Apology for Slavery?

Su-Jin: Daniel, you are from the United States, right?

Daniel: Yes, I am, Su-Jin. Why do you ask?

Su-Jin: Well, I've been studying about slavery in the U.S. recently, and I have some questions.

Daniel: Oh, okay. That was a very dark chapter in American history, but what are your questions?

Su-Jin: Are there any descendants of slaves living in America today?

Daniel: Yes, of course. There are many African-Americans who can trace their family tree directly back to slaves.

Su-Jin: I see. Well, are there any white Americans who know that they are descended from slave owners?

Daniel: Yes, there are many. I am ashamed to say this, but my great-great-great-grandfather was a slave owner. It's very sad but true.

Su-Jin: Oh, that's incredible! Do you know anyone descended from one of his slaves?

Daniel: No, that's not possible. Sadly, there aren't enough historical records to find them.

— As the President of the United States of America, I feel that we have a duty to pay reparations to the descendants of black slaves.
— Don't you think we've already paid them back?
— What do you mean?
— We've produced millions of black millionaires. Furthermore, we elected a black president for the first time in history! Isn't that enough?

UNIT 52 — An Apology for Slavery?

The first black African slaves arrived in America in the 1620s. The number of slaves grew dramatically, reaching a peak of about four million slaves in the mid-19th century. The United States actually split into two countries in 1861, the Union and the Confederate States, mainly over the issue of slavery. This division erupted into the Civil War, which claimed 623,000 lives and did not end until 1865. At that time, slavery was effectively abolished. The slaves were now free, but they and their descendants suffered under gross discrimination for another century, until the Civil Rights Movement of the 1960s.

In recent years, there has been a movement in the United States advocating that the U.S. government should pay "reparations," meaning financial compensation, to the descendants of slaves. Proponents argue that the wealth of the United States was greatly enhanced by the exploitation of free African-American slave labor. If the freed slaves had been paid fairly for their labor, their descendants would now control a much larger share of American wealth. As precedents for paying reparations, supporters point to the fact that the U.S. compensated Native American tribes for lands that were seized by the government. Also, the U.S. government apologized to Japanese-Americans for their internment during World War II and paid reparations of $20,000 to each survivor.

Others argue that paying reparations to African-American citizens today is an unfeasible idea. First of all, there are no slaves living today, and it would be impossible to trace the family tree of all the descendants of 19th-century slaves to specific individuals living today. Second, opponents show that, since the 1960s, the United States has spent $22 trillion to help the poorest Americans improve their financial situation. Many of those poor citizens were African-Americans who descended from slaves. Third, opponents point to African-Americans like Oprah Winfrey, who has a net worth of almost $3 billion, as examples of how discrimination has been mostly eliminated, allowing any African-American to achieve success.

What do you think?

(1) Should the United States apologize for slavery and compensate descendants of slaves?
(2) Did your country ever have a period of history when slavery was legal? How widespread was slavery?
(3) Does any country need to apologize to your country for past offenses? Why or why not?
(4) Does your country need to apologize to any groups of people? Why or why not?
(5) Is there any discrimination against minority groups in your country today?
(6) To what extent should the government help the poor in your country?
(7) Do you think slavery exists anywhere in the world today?

OPEN TO DEBATE 2

UNIT 53

Climate Change

Matthew: Hello Ha-Eun. What do you have in that bag?

Ha-Eun: Hi Matthew. I just bought some new light bulbs.

Matthew: Oh? What kind of light bulbs?

Ha-Eun: They are called compact fluorescent light bulbs, or CFLs.

Matthew: Are they better than the traditional type of light bulb?

Ha-Eun: Absolutely! They are more energy efficient, so they save money.

Matthew: Well, that's always good.

Ha-Eun: Also, because they use less energy, they help reduce greenhouse gas emissions.

Matthew: It seems like such a small step for one person to take. However, it can certainly help.

Ha-Eun: Yes, that's true. As my mother always says, "Every little bit helps."

I'm not feeling well. I ache all over. You're harassing me with polluted air and water and cutting down all the trees. I can barely breathe. Do you call this sort of destruction "DEVELOPMENT"? How stupid are you? I can't survive unless you stop this kind of harrowing destruction immediately.

The Doomsday Clock is ticking! Let's leave and find a new colony in space.

Don't worry! Our planet is strong enough to hang on for another millennium! He's just pretending to be sick.

UNIT 53   Climate Change

The term "climate change" refers to the rise in average surface temperatures on Earth. For that reason, the phenomenon is also called "global warming." Almost all scientists believe that climate change is caused primarily by the human use of fossil fuels, such as oil and coal, which release carbon dioxide and other greenhouse gases into the air. The gases that are released by human activity trap heat within the atmosphere. This added heat can have a huge effect on Earth's ecosystems, causing rising sea levels, severe weather patterns, and droughts.

According to experts, from 1880 to 2015, the Earth had warmed by about 1.7 degrees Fahrenheit (0.94 degrees Celsius). That may sound like a small number, but when you consider the fact that it is an average of the Earth's surface, it is actually quite high. The reality of global warming explains why glaciers are melting, and the oceans are rising at an accelerating rate. Researchers maintain that most of the warming in the last sixty years has been caused by the human release of greenhouse gases. If these emissions continue at the present pace, global warming could ultimately exceed 8 degrees Fahrenheit (4.4 degrees Celsius), which would make the planet incapable of supporting a large human population.

Individuals can limit their greenhouse gas emissions by changing to energy-efficient light bulbs, heating and cooling more efficiently, sealing and insulating one's home, recycling when possible, reducing water waste, and using solar panels.

A small percentage of people question the claim that climate change is due to human activity. They say that recent changes in the Earth's climate and temperature are part of the natural variations in Earth's climate that have fluctuated over millennia. Such naysayers are called "climate change deniers."

What do you think?

(1) Do you believe that climate change is real and that it is due to human activity?
(2) Do you think you have personally seen a warming of the climate during your lifetime?
(3) Some people say, "The summers are getting longer, and the winters are getting shorter." Do you agree?
(4) Do you know any "climate change deniers"? What arguments do they present?
(5) Are you familiar with the Kyoto Protocol? Has your country signed the agreement?
(6) Is your government doing anything to reduce greenhouse gas emissions?
(7) What are you doing personally to reduce your greenhouse gas emissions?

OPEN TO **DEBATE 2**

UNIT 54

The British Monarchy

Alexis: Jae-Hwa, I've just seen an amazing ceremony!

Jae-Hwa: Oh? What was that?

Alexis: I was at Deoksugung in Seoul, and I saw the ceremony of the Changing of the Royal Guard.

Jae-Hwa: Oh, yes. That's a very impressive ceremony. Visitors to Seoul really enjoy it.

Alexis: I can easily see why. When did this ceremony begin?

Jae-Hwa: Well, the ancient version took place during the Joseon Dynasty, but the modern version started in 1996.

Alexis: I see. How did the government ensure that the modern ceremony was accurate?

Jae-Hwa: Well, some leading Korean historians conducted extensive research before the ceremony became an institution.

Alexis: Interesting. Are there any descendants of Korean royalty still around?

Jae-Hwa: Yes, there are some alive today, but of course, they have no throne and no royal power.

Alexis: Okay. Thanks for your explanation.

I'm sick and tired of parading down the street like this every day for tourists to gawk at. I want to resign!

No way! Then who will employ us? We'll be jobless!

Your Majesty! It is such a great honor to see you! Can I take a picture of you?

UNIT 54 — The British Monarchy

In June 2015, it was announced that Buckingham Palace, the London residence and administrative headquarters of Queen Elizabeth II, was in need of repair. The massive structure contains 775 rooms, 240 of which are bedrooms. The building had not been remodeled in years and was in serious need of repairs that would require expenditures of £150m. Critics of the monarchy called again for its abolishment. They pointed out that, apart from the huge cost of maintaining the royal buildings, there is the cost of providing for the members of the royal family. According to one estimate, the royals cost the British public a total of £334m per year, which is an average of £18.5m per head. This lofty sum means that the royals are the most expensive public officials in the country. Critics say that the huge sums of money needed to maintain the royalty could be better spent on education, police, and health services. Opponents of the monarchy also argue that it is an anachronism to have an unelected head of state in the 21st century. Also, the monarchy is tied to the Church of England, which is effectively the state religion. This situation is also anachronistic since less than 10% of the population attends church.

Supporters of the monarchy say that the monarchy is cost-effective. The royal institutions attract millions of tourists each year, and tourists spend more money that the monarchy costs. The queen is also a non-partisan head of state. If the government ever started to become oppressive, the ruling monarch could step in and veto any ill-conceived proposals. Finally, every country needs a head of state. If the monarchy were abolished, the citizens would have to elect a head of state. Many British citizens fear that an undesirable leader might be elected. Perhaps that is why a poll taken in 2015 showed that 71% of British citizens want the monarchy to continue.

What do you think?

(1) If you were a British citizen, would you support the continuation of the monarchy? Why or why not?
(2) Are you interested in reading about the British royal family members?
(3) Do you have a favorite member of the British royal family?
(4) Are there any governmental institutions in your country that you would like to see abolished?
(5) In your country, which branches of government are the most important, in your opinion?
(6) Would you ever consider becoming a politician? Why or why not?
(7) Have you ever seen the changing of the guard at Buckingham Palace? Does your country have a similar ceremony?

OPEN TO DEBATE 2

UNIT 55

Climbing Mount Everest

Su-Min: Logan, do you have any plans for the weekend?

Logan: Actually, I do, Su-Min. I'm going to climb a mountain.

Su-Min: Oh, really? Which mountain are you climbing?

Logan: Bukhan Mountain. Some of my Korean students invited me to climb with them.

Su-Min: Well, since you live in Seoul, you won't have far to go.

Logan: That's right. I've been living in Korea now, and I think it's time to climb one of Korea's many mountains.

Su-Min: Well, as I'm sure you know, mountain climbing and hiking are popular sports here, especially since 70% of the country consists of mountains.

Logan: Yes, I read about that. I want to start out with a mountain that's not too challenging.

Su-Min: Well, there are three major peaks of Bukhan. Which one will you climb?

Logan: I think we'll be climbing the tallest peak, which is Baegundae, at 836.5 meters.

Su-Min: Okay. Sounds great! Have a good time and stay safe!

- Hurry up! Who are you talking to?
- I'm so happy I'm almost there!
- I can't hold on any longer! I wish I were at home!

- I'm the god of this mountain, and this is my residence! Stop disturbing my tranquility! Go down immediately!
- No way! I paid $25,000 for this climb! And I have to take a selfie on the summit.
- If you don't follow my advice, I will punish you!
- Punish me? What punishment could you give?
- An avalanche will bury you all!

UNIT 55 — Climbing Mount Everest

Back in the 1920s, George Leigh Mallory, an English mountaineer, was asked, "Why do you want to climb Mount Everest." He replied, "Because it's there." That statement has been called "the most famous three words in mountaineering." Unfortunately, it is not known whether Mallory was actually able to reach the top of Everest, the world's highest mountain. During his 1924 expedition, Mallory and his climbing partner, Sandy Irvine, both disappeared on the Northeast Ridge when they were only 245 meters from the summit. Mallory's fate was unknown for 75 years, until his body was discovered on May 1, 1999, by an expedition that set out to find the remains of the two climbers. However, the expedition was unable to find Irvine's body.

It was left to the New Zealand mountaineer, Edmund Hillary, and his Nepalese guide, Tenzing Norgay, to become the first climbers to reach the summit of Mount Everest, on May 29, 1953. Since that date, over 4,000 individuals have successfully climbed Mount Everest, and about 265 have died in the attempt. Climbing the mountain has become a huge business, and a climbing permit alone costs $25,000 per person. Researchers keep Olympic-style records of every kind of statistic you can imagine about Mount Everest. These would include the following: the youngest climber (Jordan Romero, age 13), the oldest climber (Min Bahadur Sherchan, age 76), the most deaths in one day (18 on April 26, 2015), the first blind person (Erik Weihenmayer), and many other statistics.

Unfortunately, the many climbs up the world's tallest mountain have caused critical ecological damage. The routes up the mountain are littered with oxygen canisters, broken equipment, trash, human waste, and even dead bodies. Experts estimate that tons of trash remain on the mountain. Recently, the Nepali government created a new rule that requires each climber to bring back 18 pounds of trash off the mountain. If they fail to do so, they forfeit a $4,000 deposit.

What do you think?

(1) Why do so many people want to climb Mount Everest, even though it might cost them their lives?
(2) Have you ever thought about climbing Mount Everest? Would you try to climb it if a rich friend paid your way?
(3) Some experts are urging that Mount Everest be turned into a memorial and that all climbs be banned. Do you agree with this idea?
(4) Have any individuals from your country ever climbed Mount Everest? Who were they?
(5) What is the best way to remove all the trash on Mount Everest?
(6) What is the highest mountain in your country? Have you ever climbed it?
(7) How many mountains have you climbed during your life? Why did you climb them?

OPEN TO DEBATE 2

UNIT 56

World Religions

Zachary: Ye-Ji, do you have a religion?

Ye-Ji: Yes, I do. I am a Buddhist. However, I'm not an active Buddhist. What about you?

Zachary: Well, I'm a Christian, but like you, I'm not very active.

Ye-Ji: I'm curious. Which country has the highest percentage of Christians?

Zachary: Well, the answer might surprise you. I know a country that is 100% Christian.

Ye-Ji: Are you serious? I think it's impossible to have a 100% Christian population.

Zachary: No, it's absolutely true. Every inhabitant of Vatican City is a Christian.

Ye-Ji: Haha. That's the headquarters of the Catholic Church and not a true country.

Zachary: No, it's recognized by the United Nations as an independent state.

Ye-Ji: Hmmm... okay, but I bet you can't name another one.

Zachary: Well, there is the territory of the Pitcairn Islands. All 56 residents are Christians and members of the Seventh Day Adventist Church.

Ye-Ji: Incredible! You sound like a walking encyclopedia of religion!

Science and religion shake hands for the welfare of mankind. They are no longer rivals but friends. We promise to respect each other and understand each other. Remember the words of Einstein: "Science without religion is lame; religion without science is blind."

UNIT 56 World Religions

Have you ever wondered about what percentage of people around the world believe in the existence of God? As you might imagine, answering this question is very difficult. However, a global study, conducted by the Pew Research Center in 2012, may provide some answers. The study surveyed people in 230 countries and territories and concluded that 84% of the world's population is affiliated with a religion, leaving 16% being not affiliated with a religion. However, even among the unaffiliated group, many people still have religious beliefs and practices, which may not be associated with a particular religion. In the United States, a poll taken in 2013 showed that about 75% of adults said that they believed in God, which was lower than the 82% who said the same in 2005, 2007, and 2009.

Some scientists have argued that science has shown that the idea of a divine creator and spirit is untenable. Therefore, no scientifically-minded person should believe in God. If this claim is true, we would expect that most scientists themselves would be atheists. It is interesting to compare an early survey on this question with a more recent one. In 1916, a total of 1,000 leading American scientists were asked if they believed in the existence of God. The results indicated that 41.8% believed in the existence of God, 41.5% disbelieved, and 16.7% had doubts/did not know. The same poll was taken 80 years later, and the results were almost the same. Taken in 1996, the poll indicated that 39.3% believed in God's existence, 45.3% disbelieved, and 14.5% had doubts/did not know.

The current global religious landscape shows that the largest world religions are as follows, arranged according to number of adherents and percentage of world population:

• 2.2 billion Christians (32%)	• 500 million Buddhists (7%)
• 1.6 billion Muslims (23%)	• 400 million people (6%) practicing folk or traditional religions
• 1 billion Hindus (15%)	

What do you think?

(1) Do you believe that being scientifically-minded means that you must be an atheist?
(2) Can you name any famous atheists? What are they famous for?
(3) Do you think that the topic of world religions is an interesting one to study? Why or why not?
(4) Can you identify one major belief of Christianity, Islam, Hinduism, and Buddhism?
(5) Do you believe that religion has too much power in the world?
(6) In the U.S., it would be impossible for an atheist to be elected as president. Is that true in your country?
(7) Albert Einstein said, "Science without religion is lame; religion without science is blind." What did he mean? Do you agree?

OPEN TO DEBATE 2

UNIT 57

Scientology

Chung-Ho: Madison, I'd like to invite you to my church. We're having a special series of services.

Madison: Well, Chung-Ho, thank you for the invitation, but I'm afraid that I'm not a suitable person to invite.

Chung-Ho: What do you mean?

Madison: Well, I decided a long time ago that I am an agnostic when it comes to religion.

Chung-Ho: Is that the same thing as an atheist?

Madison: No, it's not. An atheist believes that God does not exist; an agnostic simply doesn't know if God exists.

Chung-Ho: Oh, I see. So you don't know if there is a God.

Madison: Yes, that's right. I believe in science, and you can neither prove nor disprove the existence of God through scientific evidence.

Chung-Ho: Okay. So you just don't have a religion?

Madison: No, I don't. I respect all religions, and many people believe their religion helps them, but it's not for me.

Chung-Ho: Okay. I understand your position.

If I play God saying, "I'm the messenger of God," people seem to believe it. They respect me and give me a lot of money. Scientology is the purest religion in the world! Don't you know Tom Cruise is a scientology enthusiast? And he is both famous and rich!

Ridiculous! I don't have to play God and shout "I'm the messenger of God." I just sit here, and people give me money. I know they regard me as a representative of God. Why else would they give me money?

People call me a pet dog. But I think I'm actually their god. They feed me when I'm hungry, bathe me when I'm dirty, treat me when I'm sick, and always love me unconditionally. What name can I call myself except god? Furthermore, if people treated me badly they would go to jail for animal cruelty!

UNIT 57 Scientology

What is the Church of Scientology? Its celebrity members Tom Cruise and John Travolta might give you one answer. However, another type of answer comes from a former member, Jenna Miscavige Hill, who is also a niece of the current leader of the Church of Scientology, David Miscavige. Jenna's grandfather joined Scientology in the late 1960s, only a short time after L. Ron Hubbard had founded the organization in 1953. Jenna's father was a member of a group of Scientologists referred to as "the Sea Org." This group is composed of the most dedicated and elite members of the church, who are entrusted with the international management of Scientology. Joining the Sea Org requires a lifetime commitment to the church.

Early in her life, Jenna became accustomed to rarely seeing her parents, both of whom worked incredibly long hours for the Sea Org. On one occasion, when Jenna was four years old, she caught her leg in a parking gate, leaving her with a broken knee. However, her parents were still expected to report for work, and they could not ask for time off. They could only give her a bandage and leave for work. At age five, she was moved to a ranch in the California desert, where a workforce of children was remodeling the place, often working 14-hour days to complete the task.

Eventually, Jenna's parents became fed up with Scientology and left the church. However, Jenna remained. In due time, Jenna came to the conclusion that the church was all about indoctrination and control. In 2013, she published a tell-all book about her years spent in the religion. The full title of the book is revealing: *Beyond Belief: My Secret Life Inside Scientology and My Harrowing Escape*. She wrote, "To me, the Church is a dangerous organization whose beliefs allow it to commit crimes against humanity and violate basic human rights. It remains a mystery to me how, in our current society, this can go on unchecked." With other ex-church members, she launched the website exscientologykids.com.

What do you think?

(1) Are you familiar with the Church of Scientology? Do you think that it is a cult?
(2) Are there any religious cults in your country? What are they?
(3) What are the characteristics of a religious cult?
(4) Are you a member of any organized religion? How often do you participate in religious services?
(5) How would you respond if your children joined a religious cult?
(6) Would you ever marry someone who had a different religion than you?
(7) What are the best ways that religion can help society?

OPEN TO DEBATE 2

UNIT 58

China versus the United States

Elijah: Hi Ye-Lim. Where are you going?

Ye-Lim: Oh, hi Elijah. I'm going to my Chinese class.

Elijah: Oh, wow! You are studying Chinese now. That's great!

Ye-Lim: Well, I'm just a beginner, but I hope to reach intermediate level after a year of study.

Elijah: That's awesome, but it must be very difficult.

Ye-Lim: Yes, it's difficult, but I learned a lot of Chinese characters when I was in high school.

Elijah: Oh, yeah. A lot of Korean words are based on Chinese characters.

Ye-Lim: Yes, that's true, so I had a head start based on my high school studies.

Elijah: Well, as an English speaker, I think that Chinese would be very difficult for me to learn.

Ye-Lim: Yes, I heard that it's difficult for English speakers.

Elijah: Yes, difficult but not impossible. Maybe I will take some Chinese classes myself.

Ye-Lim: Oh, I hope you do. Maybe we can converse in Chinese someday.

Not yet! You aren't strong enough to knock me out of first place. Don't you see I have state-of-the-art products like iPhones and Boeing airplanes that you don't have?

Hey, Chinese! Don't try to accomplish a "MISSION IMPOSSIBLE." I tried to surpass America in the 70s and 80s, only to fail. Don't bite off more than you can chew!

Hey, American! Get off your pedestal! Now I'm the number one country in the world!

UNIT 58 — China versus the United States

In the contemporary world, there are two countries that have emerged as global major competitors: the United States and China. They have the world's largest economies and most expansive militaries, and their smallest decisions can dramatically affect the politics and economies of other countries. Despite an extensive trade agreement and frequent diplomatic meetings, China and the U.S. struggle to maintain a civil, working relationship. The following chart shows a comparison between the two superpowers in major areas (Most statistics are from 2013).

Area	United States	China
GDP	$16.72 trillion	$13.39 trillion
GDP per capita	$52,800	$9,800
Military Expenditures	4.06% of GDP	4.3% of GDP
Military Force	1.5 million	2.3 million

Area	United States	China
Literacy	99%	92%
Press Freedom	10th worldwide	139th worldwide
Economic Freedom	4th worldwide	118th worldwide
Citizens in prison (per 100,000)	730 (1st worldwide)	121 (124th worldwide)

Although the U.S. has an edge in overall GDP, in terms of Purchasing Power Parity (PPP), China now ranks as the world's largest economy, according to the International Monetary Fund. PPP enables you to see how much you can buy for your money in various countries.

The comparisons listed above do not reveal one other major area of competition between the U.S. and China: strategic power. For decades, Japan, China, and other countries accepted the U.S. as the primary strategic power in Asia. However, in recent years, China has shown that it will no longer accept the status quo and that it wants to replace the U.S. as the dominant power in Asia. Experts say that, because of China's rising power, it will be impossible for the old order to be maintained forever. Therefore, leaders of Asian countries should figure out a way for the transformation of regional power to be conducted in a peaceful manner. As China exercises more power in the South China Sea, they are deliberately creating situations that will expose how far the U.S. will go in protecting its allies in Asia. Many experts say that China seems to be winning so far.

What do you think?

(1) Do any of the statistics about the two countries surprise you?
(2) How likely is war to break out between China and the U.S. over control of the South China Sea?
(3) How would you describe the relationship of your country to the U.S.? How about to China?
(4) Which country would you prefer as the primary strategic power in Asia?
(5) Can you think of other ways in which China has shown its power in Asia?
(6) Will Chinese eventually replace English as the global language? When will this happen?
(7) Have you ever studied the Chinese language? Would you like to? What can you say in Chinese?

OPEN TO DEBATE 2

UNIT 59

Illegal Immigration to the U.S.

Savannah: Yung-Jin, I heard that you're planning to study in the United States this coming fall.

Yung-Jin: Yes, that's right. I'll be studying tourism at the University of Nevada at Las Vegas.

Savannah: Wow! That's a great school for that major.

Yung-Jin: Yeah, I know. The school is surrounded by huge hotels and casinos, so they can offer the best education in the tourism and hospitality industry.

Savannah: Well, it sounds as though you have checked everything out.

Yung-Jin: Yes, everything is ready, except for my student visa. I'm still waiting for approval.

Savannah: Oh, well make sure that you do all the paperwork correctly. That's very important.

Yung-Jin: Yeah, I know.

Savannah: If you overstay your visa, for example, you could be banned for years.

Yung-Jin: Don't worry, Savannah. I have an American consultant who is helping me with all the documents.

Savannah: Okay. That sounds great. Enjoy your study and don't spend too much time in the casinos!

Yung-Jin: Don't worry. I don't ever gamble.

This is the wall that I've made with the bricks of patriotism. It's strong and high enough to keep illegal immigrants out of our country. It will keep our country safe and secure!

Your patriotism is just a euphemism for hatred and prejudice. You've forgotten that your grandfather, mother, and wife were all immigrants to America! Get out of my way! I have to bulldoze this wall for the betterment of mankind.

UNIT 59 Illegal Immigration to the U.S.

On June 3, 2016, McKinney Boyd High School in McKinney, Texas, held its annual graduation ceremony, but the speech made by the valedictorian was anything but normal. Larissa Martinez, the top student in the senior class proclaimed in her graduation speech, "I am one of the 11 million undocumented immigrants living in the shadows of the United States. I decided to stand before you today and reveal these unexpected realities, because this might be my only chance to convey the truth to all of you that undocumented immigrants are people, too." She told her classmates that all immigrants, including undocumented ones, have dreams and hopes and want to contribute to making America great, but without a wall "built on hate and prejudice." The latter expression referred to the promise of presidential candidate Donald Trump who had stated that he wanted to build a wall between the U.S. and Mexico. Martinez also mentioned that she would be heading to Yale University in the fall. She expressed her frustration that she had tried her best to become a U.S. citizen but had waited seven years for her application to be processed. Her experience showed her that "the U.S. immigration system is broken."

Statistics from the U.S. Department of Homeland Security indicate that Larissa is one of an estimated 11.3 million unauthorized immigrants living in the United States. The number peaked at around 12 million in 2007 but has gradually declined to around 11 million. Unauthorized or undocumented immigrants make up about 5.1% of the U.S. labor force. In 2014, President Obama grew tired of Congress's failure to enact comprehensive immigration legislation, and he announced a set of executive actions that would extend temporary legal status to nearly half of the illegal immigrants in the U.S. However, in June 2016, the Supreme Court overruled Obama's executive actions, once again leaving millions of immigrants in legal limbo.

What do you think?

(1) Was it a good idea for Larissa Martinez to mention in her speech that she was undocumented? Why or why not?
(2) One U.S. presidential said he would expel all 11 million undocumented immigrants. Do you think that is a good idea or even possible?
(3) In the U.S., undocumented workers take jobs that Americans will not. Should those workers be allowed to stay?
(4) Does your country have a problem with illegal immigration? What countries are those immigrants from?
(5) Should companies that hire illegal immigrants be punished? What sort of punishment should they receive?
(6) Have you ever met an undocumented immigrant? What sort of work or study were they doing?
(7) Korea and Japan suffer from a low birth rate. Could increased immigration help solve that problem?

OPEN TO DEBATE 2

UNIT 60

The Death Penalty

Ji-Eun: Thomas, you are from the United States, right?

Thomas: Yes, I am. Why do you ask?

Ji-Eun: I am curious about the death penalty there. Is it used often?

Thomas: Since 1976, there have been 1,436 people executed.

Ji-Eun: Wow that seems like a lot! How are people executed?

Thomas: Most of them are executed by lethal injection. However, electrocution is also used.

Ji-Eun: Oh, that sounds terrible!

Thomas: I agree. That's why I am totally opposed to the death penalty.

Ji-Eun: What can you do to stop it?

Thomas: Well, I can vote for politicians who are in favor of abolishing it. A total of 19 states have already banned it.

Ji-Eun: Well, that sounds like a step in the right direction.

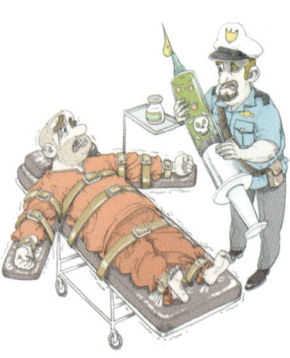

— Why are you hesitating? Go ahead! Put me out of my misery!
— You'll have to wait. We need to get some more lethal chemicals.
— I'm scared stiff from all this waiting! Why don't you just hang me? It's quicker.
— No way! That's too cruel, and nobody wants to put the rope around your neck.
— Then use the electric chair!
— That's too inhumane, and besides, we don't have an uninterruptible power supply.
— Then put me before a firing squad!
— That's too brutal, and all the sharpshooters are on leave now.

UNIT 60 — The Death Penalty

Is the United States approaching the end of the death penalty (capital punishment)? It is becoming increasingly difficult to obtain new supplies of the drugs used for lethal injections, as pharmaceutical drug companies from both Europe and the U.S. refuse to manufacture and supply such drugs. What is a state government going to do without the chemicals necessary for lethal injections? Some proponents of capital punishment have suggested bringing back the electric chair. In Virginia, for example, the primary method of execution is lethal injection. However, a condemned person can choose the electric chair if he prefers. In fact, the last use of the electric chair in the United States took place in Virginia, in 2013. In light of the difficulty in obtaining the chemicals necessary for lethal injections, the Virginia State House and Senate voted in early 2016 to restore the electric chair as the primary form of capital punishment. However, the governor rejected the bill, stating that the use of the electric chair was cruel and reprehensible. The governor proposed having American pharmaceutical companies supply the lethal drugs but keeping their names and participation secret. So far, the governor has been unsuccessful in this approach.

While it is becoming more difficult to obtain the chemicals for lethal injections, there is also increasing opposition to the death penalty by Americans. A poll taken in 1994 found that 80% of Americans supported the death penalty. However, by October 2015, the level of support had fallen to 61%. The number of executions is also decreasing. There was a high of 98 executions in 1999, 52 in 2009, and only 28 in 2015.

Critics of the death penalty say that it is used unfairly against minorities, it puts innocent lives at risk (DNA has proven some death row inmates to be innocent), it is applied randomly, it does not deter crime, and a life sentence without parole is a better alternative.

What do you think?

(1) There is no death penalty in the EU. Do you think the U.S. will soon move to this policy?
(2) If you moved to the U.S., would you prefer to live in a death penalty state (31 states) or where it is prohibited (19 states)?
(3) Does your country have the death penalty? How often is it used?
(4) If you support the death penalty, in what cases should it be used?
(5) In your country, do rich people get more favorable treatment by the justice system than poor people?
(6) In your country, if a criminal receives a life sentence, can he be released for good behavior after a certain number of years?
(7) Anton Chekhov said, "The state is not God. It has not the right to take away what it cannot restore when it wants to." What did he mean? Do you agree?

OPEN TO DEBATE 2

UNIT 61

Religious Veils in Public Places

Jasmine: Sang-Min, you're a Buddhist, right?

Sang-Min: Yes, I am. Why do you ask?

Jasmine: Well, I've been living in Korea now for a year, but I've never seen a religious service in a Buddhist temple.

Sang-Min: Are you Buddhist?

Jasmine: No, I'm not. I'm a Christian, but I'm open-minded, and I respect all religions. I would just like to see a real service at a temple.

Sang-Min: I see. Well, would you like to join my family sometime when we go to the temple?

Jasmine: Oh, that would be wonderful. Is there any special clothing that is required? Would I have to wear a veil or covering?

Sang-Min: No, there's no special clothing required. We just dress nicely and conservatively.

Jasmine: I see. Well, please let me know when I can join you.

Sang-Min: Okay. I'll talk to my parents and let you know.

— You're under arrest.
— Why? I didn't do anything wrong!
— Don't you know that wearing a veil in public places is illegal?
— The man on the motorcycle is wearing a head covering too!
— That's a helmet, and it's required by law for safety.
— I wear the veil for the same purpose: SAFETY!
— What do you mean?
— If I wear it, Muhammad will protect me under any circumstances!

UNIT 61 Religious Veils in Public Places

It is well-known that France has a large Muslim population. In fact, Muslims in France comprise about 5-10% of the national population, which means that France has the largest number of Muslims in Western Europe. Islam is the second-most common religion in France after Catholic Christianity. Of course, France maintains religious freedom, but such freedom has its limitations. In June 2009, President Nicolas Sarkozy stated publicly that religious face veils that cover the entire face, such as the niqab and burka, were "not welcome" within France. Sarkozy argued that a law was needed to protect women from being forced to cover their faces and to protect France's status as a secular country. Also, no one's face should be hidden as a matter of public security.

A national survey showed that 80% of French voters supported the ban on facial veils. In fact, out of 5,000,000 Muslims living in France, only 2,000 actually wore the facial veil, indicating that its use was a minority practice even within Islam. A law banning facial veils was passed by the French Parliament and came into effect on April 11, 2011. The law prescribed a fine of 150 Euros for anyone who violated the ban. Some face coverings, such as motorcycle helmets, were exempted from the ban. In response, hundreds of people demonstrated in Pakistan and demanded that the United Nations take action. Also, Amnesty International condemned the passage of the ban as a violation of religious freedom of expression.

The new law was challenged almost immediately by a 24-year-old French woman who claimed that the ban on wearing veils in public violated her freedom of religion and expression. However, the European Court of Human Rights upheld the French law. The Court stated that the ban "was not based on the religious connotation of the clothing in question but solely on the fact that it concealed the face."

What do you think?

(1) Do you think that the French ban on facial veils was a wise idea?
(2) Shouldn't religious people be allowed complete freedom for their personal religious expression?
(3) What are the laws in your country regarding facial veils?
(4) Have you ever seen a woman wearing a veil that covered her entire face? What did you think?
(5) What are some other types of religious clothing that you have seen?
(6) Have you personally ever worn any special type of religious clothing? What was it?
(7) What do you think is appropriate clothing to wear to a religious service?

OPEN TO DEBATE 2

UNIT 62

Women's Rights in Saudi Arabia

Samuel: So-Hee, you look so happy today. Did you get some good news?

So-Hee: Yes, I did! I passed my driver's test! Now I have a driver's license.

Samuel: Wow, that's great! Congratulations! Was the test difficult?

So-Hee: Actually, I was a little nervous, but I made all the turns and stops correctly.

Samuel: Well, I'm happy for you. You are lucky to live in Korea. In some countries, women are not allowed to drive.

So-Hee: I can't imagine that.

Samuel: By the way, now that you have a driver's license, when are you going to take me for a ride?

So-Hee: I will be happy to take you for a ride—when I get a car. At the moment, I don't have one.

Samuel: I see. Well, I'll take a rain check on that promise.

— What are you doing?
— I'm practicing driving with this video game!
— Don't you know women are not allowed to drive in our country?
— I know. But I'm preparing for my future! I'm sure the day will come when women can drive.
— Oh, don't start a trend. If word gets around, the government will prohibit this game.

UNIT 62 — Women's Rights in Saudi Arabia

In early 2016, a Starbucks coffee shop in Riyadh, Saudi Arabia, needed some renovations. Normally, there was a wall in the shop that separated male and female customers. Since the wall had to be removed for the renovations, the manager of the coffee shop placed a sign in the window that read: "Please, no entry for ladies; only send your driver to order. Thank you." The sign highlighted two rules of Saudi society that most people around the world will find shocking: Women must have a man to drive them, and men and women must sit separately when they are in public places. A religious police squad ensures that the rules are enforced.

While Saudi women were allowed to vote in municipal elections in 2015 for the first time, women's rights remain severely restricted compared to the rest of the world. In Saudi Arabia, a woman cannot open a bank account without her husband's permission. Women cannot go anywhere without a male guardian called a *mahram*, who is usually a male relative. In one extreme case, cited by the *Washington Post*, a teenager reported to police that she had been gang-raped. However, since she was not with a *mahram* at the time, she was punished by the court and was actually given more lashes than one of her alleged rapists.

The Saudi government recently announced that it was considering lifting the ban on female drivers, but any such change of policy would still have to be approved by the conservative body of senior religious leaders. These senior clerics typically argue that allowing female drivers would undermine traditional social values. In 2011, a group of Saudi women challenged the ban against female drivers by encouraging women to ignore the laws and post photos on social media of themselves driving. The response by women was very meager, and the campaign could not be considered a success.

What do you think?

(1) Was there ever a time in the history of your country when women could not drive?
(2) What are some past restrictions of women's rights that were in effect in your country (e.g., no voting)?
(3) Are there any restrictions of women's rights that still exist in your country today?
(4) Are women in your country paid the same amount as a man for doing the same type of job?
(5) What percentage of the top CEOs in your country are women?
(6) Have you ever visited a country in the Middle East? What was your impression?
(7) In your opinion, who are safer drivers, men or women?

OPEN TO **DEBATE 2**

OPEN TO DEBATE 2

UNIT 63

Indian Housewives: Shocking Rate of Suicide

Hye-Min: Andrew, I have some big news!

Andrew: Really? What's that?

Hye-Min: I'm getting married!

Andrew: Wow! That's exciting. You must be very happy.

Hye-Min: Yes, it's great. I've waited a long time. I'm almost 30 years old.

Andrew: Oh, that's not so old. By the way, how did you meet your husband?

Hye-Min: Well, my mother suggested that I meet him because he's the son of a good friend of hers.

Andrew: Hmmm... is that an arranged marriage, like they have in India and other countries?

Hye-Min: No, it's just a suggestion. We call this custom *seon*. It just means that our family members think we would be a good match.

Andrew: I see. So either of you could still refuse, right?

Hye-Min: Yes, of course, but we both sensed that we were a good match, so we moved forward in the relationship.

— Today is the last day with you, Honey. Goodbye!
— What are you doing? Are you going to hang yourself? Don't do that!
— I feel helpless! Nobody loves me, understands me, or supports me....There's no reason to live anymore.
— I feel helpless too! But I'll never take my life.
— Why not?
— I love myself so much that I can OVERCOME any difficulties!

UNIT 63 Indian Housewives: Shocking Rate of Suicide

More than 20,000 housewives in India took their own lives in 2014. In fact, since record-keeping began in 1997, the number of such suicides has topped 20,000 every year. The number peaked in 2009 with 25,092 deaths. Though suicides by farmers often make the headlines, the number of housewives who commit suicide is usually twice as high. Unfortunately, there are few studies that have tried to analyze the reasons for these shocking statistics. However, Professor Peter Mayer of the University of Adelaide has conducted substantial research on this question and published his conclusions in a book entitled *Suicide and Society in India*.

Mayer's research produced several important observations. First, female suicide rates in India are lower in "traditional" states, where families are large and extended. Rates are higher in states where families are smaller and nuclear in nature. Second, the risk of suicide is highest in the first or second decade of marriage, among women aged between 30 and 45. Third, in spite of the fact that being educated and having smaller families are situations usually associated with empowerment of women, in India, those groups actually have higher suicide rates.

Mayer's research led him to the conclusion that the shocking rate of suicide among Indian women was due to the transformation of the nature of the family that is taking place in modern India. Often, there is a rocky relationship between a well-educated young wife and her poorly educated mother-in-law. Also, many Indian women are married through arranged marriages. They may have dreams of accomplishing great things, but their husbands and in-laws do not support them, and often neither do their own parents. Also, the lack of a romantic, supportive, and affectionate relationship with her husband can lead an Indian wife to take her own life. To compound the problem, there is a lack of mental health treatment facilities and counselors.

What do you think?

(1) Is the suicide rate in your country high or low compared to other countries?
(2) In your country, what segments of society are most at risk for suicide (college students, businesspersons, housewives, etc.)?
(3) Are arranged marriages common in your country? Were they common in the past?
(4) Can you think of any benefits to having an arranged marriage?
(5) Do you personally know anyone who has had an arranged marriage?
(6) Indian families are becoming smaller and more urbanized. Is that true in your country as well?
(7) Would you ever consider marrying someone that your parents did not approve of?

OPEN TO DEBATE 2

OPEN TO DEBATE 2

UNIT 64

Addiction to Prescription Drugs

Tyler: Ji-Yoon, my back is really bothering me today. I think I need to see a doctor.

Ji-Yoon: Well, I can help you make an appointment.

Tyler: That would be great, thanks. I think I need a strong pain killer.

Ji-Yoon: Oh, I'm not sure that you can get that sort of medicine in Korea.

Tyler: Don't you have both Western and Oriental medicine?

Ji-Yoon: Of course, but even Western doctors don't prescribe strong pain killers very much.

Tyler: How can people get pain relief then?

Ji-Yoon: Well, some people use herbal medicine or physical therapy, or as a last resort, some very mild prescribed medicines.

Tyler: I see. Well, I'll just follow the doctor's orders.

Ji-Yoon: Okay. That's good. I'll make an appointment for you now.

UNIT 64 — Addiction to Prescription Drugs

On April 21, 2016, the world lost one of its most talented singers, songwriters, and record producers. Prince Rogers Nelson, better known as Prince, died at the age of 57. It was later ruled that Prince had died from a fentanyl overdose. Fentanyl is classified as an "opioid," which is a prescription drug that produces morphine-like effects and is often used to relieve pain. After Prince died, allegations were made that he had abused prescription pain pills for years. Investigators attempted to discover how Prince could have had continuing access to such drugs that can only be prescribed by a physician.

The death of Prince was discussed on many American television talk shows and led to the discussion of a wider topic: the abuse of prescription pain killers in the United States. In fact, the U.S. Centers for Disease Control and Prevention (CDC) has officially declared that prescription drug abuse in the United States is at an epidemic level. Americans represent only about 5% of the world's population, but they consume about 80% of the pain killers prescribed in the entire world.

As of 2012, the number of annual deaths in the U.S. involving prescription opioids reached almost 17,000. Nearly 9 out of 10 poisoning deaths are caused by drugs—both illegal and prescribed. Indeed, prescribed opioid pain relievers were involved in more drug poisoning deaths than heroin and cocaine. Moreover, the increased use of prescription opioids has resulted in a devastating side effect: the use of heroin has dramatically increased as well. People become addicted to pain pills, and then, when they no longer have access to the pills, they switch to heroin, which produces a similar "high" feeling. Heroin use rose by 75% between 2007 and 2011. Many Americans are pessimistic that any progress is being made in reducing the excessive use of prescription opioids.

What do you think?

(1) Are you familiar with the music of Prince? How did you react when he died?
(2) Can you think of any other celebrities who have died because of an addiction to prescription drugs?
(3) How easy is it in your country to get a prescription for a pain killer?
(4) How easy is it in your country to buy illegal drugs?
(5) Has anyone ever tried to sell you an illegal drug?
(6) When you feel a continuous pain, how do you deal with it?
(7) Do you know of any natural, non-medicinal remedies for pain?

OPEN TO DEBATE 2

OPEN TO DEBATE 2

UNIT 65

Claiming the Arctic and Antarctic

Kaitlyn: Tae-Min, are you familiar with Korea's Exclusive Economic Zone?

Tae-Min: You mean the EEZ? I know a little about it. I'm majoring in geography.

Kaitlyn: Well, has Korea fully established its EEZ?

Tae-Min: Not exactly. South Korea claims an EEZ of 475,469 square meters, but Japan disputes part of the territory.

Kaitlyn: I see. I read that countries with overlapping EEZs are encouraged to negotiate.

Tae-Min: Yeah, that's true, but Korea and Japan can't seem to agree on their EEZs.

Kaitlyn: Well, that's too bad. It would be better for both countries to get the matter settled.

Tae-Min: True, but Japan also has disputes about EEZs with Russia, China, and Taiwan.

Kaitlyn: That's surprising. I wonder if those issues will ever be resolved.

Tae-Min: Well, Japan claims about 10 times as much territory as Korea's EEZ. I think they should just agree to Korea's claim.

Kaitlyn: Sounds reasonable to me.

Get out! This is our land because we were the first to plant our flag!

That's right. This is ours. First come, first served!

Just a moment! I'm almost there!

I'm going to fly my flag there. Why don't you move over a bit and make room for me!

It's so crowded there! I'm going to fly my flag here on an iceberg. Why don't you come over here! There are so many icebergs floating around unoccupied.

UNIT 65 — Claiming the Arctic and Antarctic

August 2, 2007, was a memorable day for flag planting. On that date, a Russian sea expedition called Arktika 2007, composed of six explorers, descended to the seabed at the North Pole. They planted the Russian flag and took water and soil samples. The claims that emerged after the exploration were unsurprising. Russia's Natural Resources Ministry stated that the research had confirmed that the eastern section of the seabed, known as the Lomonosov Ridge, was an extension of the Russian Federation's continental shelf and therefore Russian property. If the claim is upheld, Russia will be able to increase the size of its continental shelf by 1.2 million square meters and have access to approximately 10,000 billion tons of conventional fuel.

In response to the Russian claims, Canada's Foreign Affairs Minister said, "The Russians are fooling themselves if they think dropping a flag on the ocean floor is going to change anything. This isn't the 14th or 15th century." In addition to Russia and Canada, the countries of Norway, Denmark (via Greenland), and the United States all have claims to the Arctic. According to international law, the five countries that surround the Arctic are limited to an exclusive economic zone (EEZ) of 200 nautical miles (370 km) adjacent to their coasts. The waters beyond the EEZs are considered international waters. The only possible exception to this rule occurs if a country can prove how far its continental shelf extends.

The situation in the Antarctic is somewhat different. The Antarctic Treaty, written in 1959, has now been signed by 53 countries, including the United Kingdom, the United States, the now-defunct Soviet Union, and both North and South Korea. This agreement established the Antarctic as a place of scientific research and banned all military activity in that area. However, the Antarctic holds abundant mineral deposits and energy reserves, including billions of tons of coal. In recent years, some nations, including the U.K., have sought to extend their territory.

What do you think?

(1) Should some nations be allowed to use the Arctic and Antarctic as sources of energy in the future?
(2) Should smaller nations insist that they be allowed to establish bases in the Arctic and Antarctic?
(3) Do you believe that the United Nations can effectively supervise the Polar Regions?
(4) Could there be a war in the future over the resources in the Polar Regions?
(5) Are there any disputes about the extent of your country's EEZ?
(6) Do you believe that all the ice around the Polar Regions could melt someday?
(7) Would you like to visit the Antarctic someday? Why or why not?

OPEN TO DEBATE 2

UNIT 66

India versus Pakistan

Noah: Su-Bin, I've been reading about the Dokto issue.

Su-Bin: Oh, that's a hot issue here in Korea.

Noah: What do you think about it?

Su-Bin: Well, like all Koreans, I think Dokto belongs to Korea.

Noah: The historical records seem very complicated to me, but I think that Korea has made a good case for ownership of Dokto.

Su-Bin: I'm happy to hear you say that.

Noah: In any case, considering that Japan invaded Korea, I think that the Japanese should just give up on the issue of Dokto.

Su-Bin: They would be smart to do that, in my opinion.

Noah: Besides, the Korean Coast Guard has administered the island since 1954.

Su-Bin: That's right. The island is effectively under Korean control.

Noah: Yeah, and I don't think Japan would ever go to war over such an issue.

Get out, Mr. Obama! This is none of your business! We have no choice but to use our nuclear weapons to settle our territorial disagreements.

Stop! Don't you realize that your dispute has put the whole world in danger? We can settle any issue at the table by dialogue!

We're willing to use nuclear weapons too. Mr. Obama, can we borrow some nuclear bombs? We're afraid our rival has more bombs than we have.

UNIT 66 — India versus Pakistan

After India was partitioned in 1947, two sovereign states were created: the Dominion of Pakistan (which later split into Pakistan and Bangladesh) and the Union of India (later called the Republic of India). Unfortunately, the division did not lead to a peaceful coexistence of the two countries. Pakistan was composed of a majority Muslim population, and India held a mostly Hindu population. The newly formed countries could not agree on the control of the princely state of Jammu and Kashmir, a conflict that continues to this day. Based on documents signed in 1947, India claims the entire state of Jammu and Kashmir, but they administer only 43% of the region. Pakistan claims the same area based on its majority Muslim population but administers approximately 37% of Kashmir. China controls other regions, based on its victories during the Sino-Indian War of 1962.

India and Pakistan have fought three wars over Kashmir: the Indo-Pakistani Wars of 1947 and 1965 and the Kargil War of 1999. According to experts, the conflict in 1999 almost erupted into a nuclear war, as both sides possess nuclear weapons. U.S. President Bill Clinton met with the Prime Minister of Pakistan to discuss the conflict, and Clinton was warned by his national security advisor that the meeting could well be "the single most important meeting with a foreign leader of his entire presidency." Fortunately, war was averted. Later, in 2002, Clinton would describe Kashmir as "the most dangerous place in the world."

In 1957, the United Nations Security Council expressed its belief that the final disposition of Jammu and Kashmir should be based on the will of the people in that region. In 2008, Barack Obama stated that he hoped to resolve the crisis between India and Pakistan. However, during his presidency, he took the more realistic view that the issue of Kashmir should be solved by bilateral talks between India and Pakistan.

What do you think?

(1) Do you think the conflict in Kashmir will be resolved during your lifetime?
(2) Would a vote of all the residents of Kashmir be a fair way to settle the conflict?
(3) Should the United Nations do more to resolve the conflict?
(4) Do you agree with the statement that Kashmir is "the most dangerous place in the world"?
(5) Does your country face any border and territorial conflicts with other countries? How should they be resolved?
(6) If you had a friend from India or Pakistan, would you discuss the Kashmir issue with them?
(7) If you had a chance to visit Kashmir, would you go?

OPEN TO DEBATE 2

UNIT 67

The Sunni and the Shia

Natalie: Jin-Woo, it seems that religious people in Korea seem to get along well. Am I correct?

Jin-Woo: Well, in general, they live together peaceably, but not always.

Natalie: Really? What do you mean?

Jin-Woo: Well, back in 1999, rival Buddhist monks of the Chogye order fought over control of the main temple in Seoul.

Natalie: Oh, yeah. I remember seeing that on TV.

Jin-Woo: It was shameful. The riot police had to come in and break up the fight.

Natalie: Well, what about Christians? They live peacefully with others, don't they?

Jin-Woo: Not entirely. Some Christians go to Buddhist temples and hold Christian services.

Natalie: That's incredible!

Jin-Woo: It's a practice called *ddangbarpgi* in Korean. They try to convert the Buddhists inside their own temple.

Natalie: That's very offensive. Every religion has a right to practice its own beliefs.

Jin-Woo: Of course, I agree with you.

Don't be scared. Buddha is in your mind. Accept your destiny with tranquility.

Are you guys crazy? We're sinking! Stop praying and start bailing out water!

Even if you don't save us, I won't blame you, because I'll be able to see you in heaven!

I'm not afraid of any storm like this. I've prayed five times every day during my life, so I'm sure that Muhammad will save me at least, even if he can't save us all.

UNIT 67 — The Sunni and the Shia

On October 14, 2014, the Shiite cleric Sheikh Nimr al-Nimr was sentenced to death by a court in Saudi Arabia. The charges leveled against al-Nimr alleged that he had sought foreign intervention in Saudi Arabia, disobeyed its rulers, and took up arms against the security forces. The arrest of al-Nimr and the subsequent sentence were sharply criticized as unjustified by Amnesty International. A spokesperson for the human rights organization stated that the death sentence was "part of a campaign by the authorities in Saudi Arabia to crush all dissent, including those defending the rights of the Kingdom's Shia Muslim community." Around January 2, 2016, al-Nimr was in fact executed. In response, Iranian protestors in Tehran ransacked the Saudi Embassy and set fire to it.

The sad fate of the Shiite cleric highlights a continuing conflict within the religion of Islam. In order to understand the clash, one must know a little background information. There are numerous branches of the Muslim religion, but the two major branches are the Sunni and the Shia. Experts estimate that 85-90% of the world's Muslims are Sunni, and 10-15% are Shia. Sunnis are the majority in most Muslim communities, including Saudi Arabia. Shias are the majority population in Iraq, Iran, Azerbaijan, and Bahrain. The largest number of Sunni Muslims are found in Indonesia, and the largest number of Shia Muslims are found in Iran.

The main reason for the split between the Sunni and Shia can be traced back to the death of Muhammad in 632. The Sunnis claim that Muhammad did not specifically appoint a successor to lead the Muslim community before his death. Thus, after the death of Muhammad, there was a period of confusion until a group of Muhammad's most prominent followers came together and elected Abu Bakr Siddique, Muhammad's close friend and a father-in-law, as the first caliph of Islam. In contrast, the Shia believe that Ali ibn Abi Talib, who was Muhammad's cousin and son-in-law, was the legitimate successor to Muhammad.

What do you think?

(1) Are you shocked that a death sentence was given to al-Nimr?
(2) Have you read much about the Sunni-Shia conflict?
(3) Has there ever been any persecution of religious minorities in your country?
(4) Are there any contemporary religious conflicts in your country?
(5) Do you see religion as a force for good in your country, or just another source of conflict?
(6) Would you like to visit Saudi Arabia or Iran? Why or why not?
(7) There are currently 49 countries in which Muslims comprise more than 50% of the population. How many of those countries can you name?

OPEN TO DEBATE 2

UNIT 68

Chemical Weapons

Ye-Jin: Austin, are you following developments in the Syrian Civil War?

Austin: Not extensively, but I see it on the news a lot.

Ye-Jin: Yeah, me too, but I have a lot of trouble indentifying who the good guys and bad guys are.

Austin: Oh, I think that everyone has that problem.

Ye-Jin: I just looked at an article on Wikipedia entitled "List of Armed Groups in the Syrian Civil War."

Austin: Oh, yeah. I've seen that article. It shows four major groups of fighters and hundreds of smaller groups.

Ye-Jin: That's right. It's impossible for the average person like me to understand this conflict.

Austin: I agree, and I don't have confidence in wishing for a particular group to be victorious.

Ye-Jin: I know exactly what you mean.

Austin: Yeah, sometimes it's just impossible to separate the good guys from the bad guys.

When chemical warfare broke out, I didn't have to worry because I was rich enough and smart enough to buy the latest gas mask. I WAS RIGHT. Now everybody has died from toxic gases except me. What should I do now? I want to move to another planet, and I still have enough money to buy a space shuttle. But I have no friends anymore. I wish I had bought gas masks for them, but it's too late! There are just some things you can't do over.

UNIT 68 Chemical Weapons

If you watch the news only sporadically, you will be aware that there is one war that continues unabated in our generation: the Syrian Civil War. It is a multi-sided armed conflict combined with international interventions. The conflict began in the spring of 2011, when nationwide protests began in Syria against the rule of President Bashar al-Assad's government. The military responded with violent crackdowns against protestors, and shortly thereafter, the dispute morphed from street protests into an armed rebellion. A United Nations report, released in December 2012, stated that the conflict included a strong religious aspect: the government's Shia forces fighting against Sunni-majority rebel groups.

As fighting intensified, allegations were made that chemical weapons were being used in the war. In March 2013, U.N. Secretary-General Ban Ki-moon established a mission to investigate 16 supposed chemical weapons attacks. In September 2013, U.N. inspectors confirmed the use of sarin gas in four cases, including in the Ghouta region of Syria, with a death toll estimated from 322 to 1,729 people. The attack was the deadliest use of chemical weapons since the Iran-Iraq War (1980-1988).

Sarin is a nerve agent, estimated to be 26 times more deadly than cyanide, and even at very low concentrations, it can be fatal. The initial symptoms of sarin exposure are a runny nose, a feeling of tightness in the chest, and constriction of the pupils of the eyes. Then the victim experiences difficulty in breathing, along with nausea and loss of control of bodily functions. After that, the victim experiences twitching and jerking before becoming comatose and dying in a series of convulsions.

Unfortunately, the U.N. fact-finding mission sent to Syria did not blame any party in the conflict for using chemical weapons. The U.S. and the E.U. accused the Syrian government of using the chemicals. However, human rights investigator Carla del Ponte accused the rebels of using the sarin gas. Because of international pressure, the destruction of chemical weapons in Syria was commenced.

What do you think?

(1) Should international forces, such as those of the U.S., Russia, and the E.U., intervene in Syria?
(2) What is the best way to end the Syrian Civil War? If you were head of the U.N., what would you do?
(3) If the perpetrators of the sarin gas attack are identified, what sort of punishment should they face?
(4) Can you think of any other wars and conflicts where chemical weapons have been used?
(5) Do you think that any of your neighboring countries possess chemical weapons? Which countries?
(6) Is your country prepared in case of a chemical weapons attack?
(7) Do you have masks at home to protect you against a chemical weapons attack?

OPEN TO DEBATE 2

OPEN TO DEBATE 2

UNIT 69

A Colony on Mars?

Mia: Jin-Soo, a group of us are watching a DVD tonight. Would you like to join us?

Jin-Soo: Well, maybe. What movie are you watching?

Mia: It's called *The Martian*, starring Matt Damon.

Jin-Soo: Oh, I've heard of that. It's supposed to be a pretty good film, isn't it?

Mia: Yes, it's excellent. It had several nominations for the Academy Awards, including Best Picture and Best Actor.

Jin-Soo: What is the basic plot of the film?

Mia: Well, Damon stars as an astronaut who is presumed dead and left behind on Mars.

Jin-Soo: Oh, that sounds ominous!

Mia: Yes, it is. The film shows his struggle to survive and his friends' efforts to rescue him.

Jin-Soo: Well, is he rescued in the end?

Mia: I can't tell you that! It would spoil the ending!

Jin-Soo: Okay. I'd like to see it. Count me in.

— They are immigrating to Mars!
— Good news! Once they have all moved to Mars, this place is ours. We can rebuild our planet, and we can live comfortably without them.
— They were so stupid to have polluted the earth! What a senseless waste!
— Men don't realize the importance of what they have until they lose it.

Don't be so sad! First we'll move to Mars, and later, if necessary, we can move to other planets. There are still billions of planets we can inhabit in space. We have destroyed just one planet!

UNIT 69 A Colony on Mars?

A human mission to the Planet Mars has been the subject of numerous books and films since the 19th century. According to NASA, a journey to Mars is possible, and they are making plans to bring it about. NASA's Program Orion projects that human beings will be able to travel to Mars as soon as 2035. NASA's plan involves three distinct stages that will culminate in a fully sustained colony on Mars. The first stage, already underway, is known as the "Earth Reliant" phase. This phase concentrates on using the International Space Station until 2024, creating deep space technologies, and studying the effects of long-term space missions on the human body. The second phase is called "Proving Ground." During this stage, scientists will operate in "cislunar space," which means within the Moon's orbit. They will test deep space modes of habitation and identify the human capabilities that will be needed for human exploration of Mars. The final phase is called the "Earth Independent" phase. It involves long-term missions to the moon where habitats for humans will be established. Assuming that all three of these phases are successful, astronauts will be ready to make the long-distance trip to Mars.

One important factor involved in a possible trip to Mars is the fact that astronauts will likely be expected to remain there. This notion is known as the "Mars to Stay" policy. Former astronaut Buzz Aldrin, who was the second man to walk on the moon, said that astronauts who travel to Mars would have to think of themselves as pioneers. He said, "If we are going to put a few people down there and ensure their appropriate safety, would you then go through all that trouble and then bring them back immediately, after a year, a year and a half?" Aldrin answers no to that question. The astronauts will have to sacrifice themselves for the betterment of mankind.

What do you think?

(1) Do you believe that NASA will send astronauts to Mars by the year 2035?
(2) Is a trip to Mars really worth spending trillions of dollars? Shouldn't that money be used to help people on Planet Earth?
(3) If you had a chance, would you travel to Mars, even if it meant staying there permanently?
(4) If you're not willing to stay on Mars, would you be willing to travel to the Moon and return to Earth?
(5) Does your country have a program for space exploration? How extensive is it?
(6) If your government had a budget surplus of one trillion dollars, should they spend it on scientific research or divide it among the citizens?
(7) Do you like science fiction films? What is your favorite?

UNIT 70

National Foods

Samantha: Hi Heon-Woo, how about some lunch?

Heon-Woo: That sounds good. Where would you like to go?

Samantha: I don't have a lot of time. How about McDonald's®?

Heon-Woo: Sure, that's fine. May I ask you a question?

Samantha: Of course. What's your question?

Heon-Woo: Do you eat a hamburger every day? You are American, right?

Samantha: Yes, I'm American, but I don't eat a hamburger every day.

Heon-Woo: Oh really? I thought that, since it's your national dish, you must eat it almost every day.

Samantha: That's a common misconception about Americans, but studies have shown that most Americans eat hamburgers about three times per week.

Heon-Woo: Oh, I would have guessed a lot more.

Samantha: Many people think that, but in my case, I only eat a hamburger about once a week.

Heon-Woo: Oh, I see.

I'm Gimbap from Korea. I have every necessary type of nutrition you need. I'm easy to make and carry, so I'm sure I'll replace every dish in the world the moment people learn about me.

I come from Italy. I'm the essence of nutrition. But I'm wrongly accused of fattening people up.

I'm the most popular food in the world. I'm so nutritious that people don't have to worry about their health if they eat me alone. Furthermore, I'm cheap and fast! But I'm sad when people call me "junk food."

I'm the Korean traditional food Kimchi! I'm healthy and harmonious with other foods. People around the world are crazy about me.

I'm a traditional American food and taste delicious. But I'm a bit expensive, so not everybody can enjoy me.

UNIT 70 National Foods

A national dish is a type of food that is strongly associated with a specific country. A particular dish could be designated as a national dish for several reasons: (1) It is a staple food, made from local foodstuffs and prepared in a unique way. For example, *sautéed reindeer* is a traditional food of Finland and other Scandinavian countries. A steak is cut from a reindeer and sliced thinly, fried in oil, spiced with pepper and salt, and cooked with some water, cream, or beer added. The dish is then served with mashed potatoes and lingonberry (mountain cranberry) preserves.

(2) A national dish can be chosen as such because it contains an exotic ingredient that is only produced locally. For instance, "ackee and saltfish" is a traditional Jamaican dish. It uses salt codfish as a base, which is sautéed with boiled ackee (a type of fruit), onions, and other ingredients, including Scotch Bonnet peppers. This type of pepper is grown in Jamaica and is used to flavor ackee and saltfish, as well as jerk chicken, another Jamaican dish.

(3) Finally, a national dish can be chosen because it is used in conjunction with a festive food tradition, a cultural heritage, or part of a religious practice. In China, noodles are important because they symbolize longevity. They are usually served on the Chinese New Year's Eve, as a way of starting the New Year with a wish for long life.

National dishes are an important part of a nation's self-image and sense of identity. Over the centuries, nations developed a national cuisine to distinguish themselves from their rivals. On the other hand, for some countries, it is impossible to choose a single national dish. Countries such as Mexico and India have such diverse ethnic populations that a single dish could not adequately represent the entire country.

What do you think?

(1) What is the national dish of your country? How often do you eat it?
(2) Does your country have more than one national dish? What other foods are considered national dishes?
(3) Does your country have a national drink made from alcohol? How often do you drink it?
(4) Do you eat any special foods during holiday periods? Do those foods have symbolic meanings?
(5) How many national dishes have you tried from other countries? What was the most unusual?
(6) Can you name the national dishes of these countries: U.S., Canada, U.K., France, Germany, Japan?
(7) What is one type of food that you would never eat? Why?

1

— What are your biggest regrets?
— I have six regrets, including five that average people have, such as not being true to myself and working too hard.
— Then what is your last one?
— I should have gotten some life insurance! Then when I die, you would have some money.
— Why don't you do it now?
— It's too late.
— Oh, no. It's never too late! I will contact the insurance company and help you get some life insurance!

2

Let's make the world safer!

The Olympics Swimming Committee is now demanding that every swimmer wear a life jacket to avoid any possibility of drowning.

In the sport of cycling, riders must use only tricycles to avoid falling down.

In the boxing ring, boxers need to take off their gloves so they don't suffer a concussion.

10

Only a small percentage of humans are victims of human trafficking while all pigs are victims of animal trafficking. It's time that humans solved the problems of animal trafficking before they tackle their own trafficking problems.

Are you kidding? It's your destiny to end up like this!

At least we should be treated and carried with decency before being slaughtered. We want to be carried in a LIMOUSINE! Is it too much to ask as our last wish?

Treated with decency? You must be kidding! You're going to be put to death in a moment!

Think of these cartoons as scenes in a movie. The dialog has been scripted. Now we need actors to play the parts.

9

— I'm always so busy doing SNS, including Facebook, Instagram, Tumbler, and Twitter! So I have no time to look for a job, to meet friends, or to feed my baby. But I'm so happy because I have a lot of "real" friends online. I'm absolutely sure they will do everything for me when I'm in trouble.
— Daddy! What're you doing? I'm starving!
— Be quiet! Don't you see I'm busy? Aren't you old enough to feed yourself?

8

— This is our block. Go away!
— What do you mean "your block"? All that food has been thrown away. We have a right to eat it if we want!
— Can't you see the sign? Dogs are not allowed here!
— That's ridiculous! That sign means "dogs are welcome!"

3

What's happening? The monitor is sucking me in! Is this good or bad? Maybe I can join the game for real!

A life of luxury is possible on the flying carpet called Facebook!

Online shopping is based on timing. I have replaced one hand with a mouse so that I can shop more quickly and less expensively!

4

You didn't yield! This is totally your fault!

Nonsense! You must be DUI. I'm going to call the police!

It's mine! I saw it first! Go away!

No way! Let's decide by flipping a coin!

S·Y·N·O·P·S·I·S

These are the pictures you've seen in this chapter. It will be good speaking practice for you to talk about these pictures once again. Your teacher will ask you "What are they doing?" or "What does this picture mean?" or some other question. You can give a straight answer or you can use your imagination. The purpose is to allow free conversation; there is no "right" answer.

5

This dog is scaring me to death! I'm going to sue the owner!

This guy's noise is driving me crazy! I'm going to sue him!

What? Another blackout? I was in the middle of my video game! I'm going to sue the power company!

Don't these problems seem frivolous? Not to these people! What seems trivial to one person is a life-and-death matter to another.

7

Don't even think about it! If you fail, you'll be put to death immediately!

— Why are you inside that cage?
— We've been kept here since we were little to produce eggs.
— That's terrible! How can you keep laying eggs there? It's like you're in jail!
— That's so true! We're miserable.
— Why don't you escape?
— How can we?
— I'll bring you a DVD entitled The Shawshank Redemption. I'm sure it'll help you.

6

Don't move and be quiet. He's drunk now, but maybe he'll be okay tomorrow.

I'm scared. We'd better call the police!

No way! It will make him even angrier, and he'll hit us instead of the punching bag.

I'm not a violent man by nature. I don't hit anyone unless they deserve it!

151

11

Don't complain! We ALWAYS treat black and white people equally. We're just LESS interested in white people's crimes.

Why are you abusing me? What did I do wrong? Why don't you arrest those two white gang members standing there?

Hooray! This is real democracy!

12

Be thankful you had a chance to participate in the greatest sport in the world! Sorry but it's time for me to take your life! Do you have any last words?

You have a sword, and I don't! How can that be fair? Why not give me a sword too? You are just a coward in a fancy costume! This is not a sport. It's just a SLAUGHTER!

20

Get out! You're a woman! You're not allowed in here!

You can't use this restroom! You're a man!

This is ridiculous! How long must I wait until the government decides which restroom I can use? This should be a very simple matter to resolve. I was born a man but look like a woman. So it should be okay for me to use either restroom as I please.

Think of these cartoons as scenes in a movie. The dialog has been scripted. Now we need actors to play the parts.

19

What counts in marriage is loving each other, respecting each other, and understanding each other, regardless of whether the union is between a man and a woman, a man and a man, or a woman and a woman. Marriage is a gift from god. When he gave us this gift, he never mentioned who should marry whom.

18

We have finally developed new technology that turns annoying spam emails into real Spam! So we welcome your spam emails 24/7. The more spam emails you send, the more Spam we can produce. We can solve both the problem of the worldwide food shortage and the problem of spam emails at the same time.

13

A gunfight in broad daylight! Where are the police?

We're scared too. Now that everybody has the freedom to bear arms, people need to take care of themselves and protect themselves with guns. We are powerless in these circumstances.

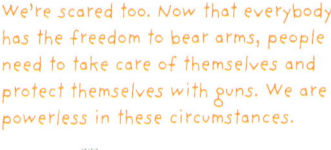

— This is a fair way to settle our differences, isn't it?
— I agree. But we used to be best friends. It's too bad that one of us has to die. Isn't there another way we could settle our disagreement?
— You make a good point. Why don't we just flip a coin?

14

— You know that I'm innocent! Let me out right now! I want a retrial!
— I know you're innocent. But a retrial is impossible until the real criminal is arrested.
— Then what will happen if the real killer is not caught?
— You will serve life in prison.
— You know I'm innocent of the crime, and you put me in prison wrongfully! Why?
— Justice must be served under any circumstances. But if the real killer is caught, you'll be set free, and you'll get a lot of money. You'll be a millionaire!
— Yeah, but it's more likely that I'll stay here for a lifetime with no compensation!
— True, but haven't you heard the old saying "No risk, no result"?

S·y·n·o·p·s·i·s

These are the pictures you've seen in this chapter. It will be good speaking practice for you to talk about these pictures once again. Your teacher will ask you "What are they doing?" or "What does this picture mean?" or some other question. You can give a straight answer or you can use your imagination. The purpose is to allow free conversation; there is no "right" answer.

15

Human females are not allowed to breast-feed their babies in public places. It's unnatural! They're living under a dictatorship!

I don't think so. It has nothing to do with the political system. They just need to seize their maternal rights.

I'm so lucky that I was born a pig. I can suck mom's nipple whenever I'm hungry!

I wish I could be a human baby, even if I'd go hungry.

17

It should be legalized right now!

No way! It should be illegal because it makes people helpless and hopeless!

Leave me alone! What matters is that I should be used PROPERLY. If well used, I can save a lot of people from painful suffering. But if I am abused, the side effects are devastating!

16

What are you talking about? I don't even like sugar! There's no reason for me to be called a "sugar daddy."

I don't like sugar either! Can't you see that I'm as slim as chopsticks? I'm not a sugar baby. We're just in love, SWEET LOVE!

You two look like a "sugar daddy-sugar baby" couple!

153

27

We're the fastest growing minority in the U.S. We deserve more admissions!

I guess I'm lucky I was born white.

I should never have written on my application that I'm Hispanic!

This is unbelievable! I'm just as qualified as any applicant!

22

Humans don't know that they should only eat octopus in the water. That's why they sometimes choke to death when they eat live octopus.

Live frog is the best dish in the world! I'm afraid that humans have discovered this too! If they know that live frogs are healthy and tasty, my species will go extinct ... as I'm about to!

I'm sick and tired of eating live mice! Roasted mice would be much tastier. Unfortunately, I don't know how to make fire!

30

In 2050, Oxford University Press decides that it will erase two words in the dictionary: the words marriage and divorce. Why? Because no one gets married anymore nor do they get divorced.

Think of these cartoons as scenes in a movie. The dialog has been scripted. Now we need actors to play the parts.

29

Because online bullying has become such a serious social problem, Samsung has introduced a very innovative smart phone. With this phone, you can't post negative statements online while remaining anonymous. Also, Apple has announced it has developed new software technology that automatically turns negative statements into positive statements. Which one is better? Do you think these smart phones are selling well?

I'm better than you! I'll be selling like hotcakes!

Nonsense! Customers will decide which one is better. Time will tell!

28

In spite of our prenup, I will love her forever. She's always been my soul mate and always will be!

I wasn't sure he was my Mr. Right. That's why I demanded we have a prenup. It'll ensure that my rights are guaranteed.

Prenuptial agreements are necessary because we don't know who is Mr. Right or Ms. Right unless we live together for a long time. But some say the fact that we make a prenuptial agreement really means that we ARE ALWAYS READY to part ways. That's our dilemma.

23

— I'm going to hit this vicious dog!
— You'd better think twice. If you hit it, you'll be arrested for cruelty to animals.
— Then what can I do about this mad dog biting me?
— Don't worry! We'll give him a warning.

Everybody is equal under the law.

24

— I feel so bad that we're dropping this nuclear bomb. So many people are going to die or suffer from radioactivity.
— You don't have to be sorry! This is the only way to end this dreadful war, and we have to follow the commander-in-chief's orders. Besides, Japan started the war!

S·Y·N·O·P·S·I·S

These are the pictures you've seen in this chapter. It will be good speaking practice for you to talk about these pictures once again. Your teacher will ask you "What are they doing?" or "What does this picture mean?" or some other question. You can give a straight answer or you can use your imagination. The purpose is to allow free conversation; there is no "right" answer.

S·Y·N·O·P·S·I·S

25

Artificial fur is much better. You don't have to wear real fur!

Fur exists for our clothing, not people's!

We're being killed every day MEANINGLESSLY for your VANITY!

27

— So finally, I've caught you red-handed! You're having a love affair! I'm going to kill you!
— Oh, please calm down! It's not my fault! I have a gene that "forces" me to have love affairs. I can't help myself!
— So, you blame it on your gene? Well, that gives me a good excuse too. If I kill you, it's my gene that forced me to kill you. I'll be innocent!

I hope the bullet won't pass through him and hit me too!

26

Appearance has nothing to do with our character. We're all humans! So there is no reason to discriminate against each other. Remember the words of Martin Luther King, Jr.: People should not be judged by the color of their skin, but by the content of their character.

31

I am the messenger of God! I'm always lobbying God to fulfill your wishes. But I need more money to do a good job.

I'm just 20. I don't need a ticket to heaven, but I want to be rich ASAP! How can I get a lot of money like you?

I'm dying. How much is a ticket to heaven? I'm willing to sell all my possessions!

32

The proliferation of drones has made cars and airplanes obsolete. But even drones will become outdated in the next century. With the help of biology, men will have wings!

40

You must be kidding! Are you envious of their marriage?

— You have three wives? That's immoral!
— What're you talking about? We're in love and our polygamous marriage is happier than yours.
— It's against God's law!
— We don't think so. Love is love regardless of what kind of marriage we have.
— Then I have a question. Even though we have a monogamous marriage, we argue a lot. What's the secret of maintaining a harmonious marriage?
— We have no time to argue with each other because we're always busy loving each other.

Think of these cartoons as scenes in a movie. The dialog has been scripted. Now we need actors to play the parts.

39

"Wow! They know we're coming soon. We're generous enough to accept their suggestion, aren't we?"

No! I want all the money!

— Congratulations! You are the winner of the $100,000,000 lottery!
— Wow! This is so exciting! Thank you so much!
— Who are you going to share all this money with?
— Oh, we'll share it with our family, friends, and relatives, and then we'll donate the rest of it. However, before that, we'll have to share it with some people who are coming to our house for the money. We'll suggest to them that we can split the money 50-50 on the condition that they spare our lives.

38

We planned this group blind date to solve the 40-year-virgin problem. You have a great chance of success because you all have at least one thing in common: you're all virgins! So there's a good possibility that you can find your perfect match right here! Good luck! Start mingling!

33

I produce silk for people. Isn't that enough? Then why do they eat our dead bodies? It's so cruel!

We always sing beautiful songs for people day and night! Then why do you want to eat us? If you keep eating us, we'll stop singing for you. Don't you know we are better than Mozart and Beethoven?

I don't know how people came to know I'm an excellent source of protein. I'm in danger of extinction!

34

What's wrong with grade inflation? It helps students get good jobs and eliminates complaints about tuition inflation among parents and students. Everybody is happy! Furthermore, according to economic theory, moderate inflation is better than deflation.

S·Y·N·O·P·S·I·S

These are the pictures you've seen in this chapter. It will be good speaking practice for you to talk about these pictures once again. Your teacher will ask you "What are they doing?" or "What does this picture mean?" or some other question. You can give a straight answer or you can use your imagination. The purpose is to allow free conversation; there is no "right" answer.

35

What a stupid decision! How unfair!

Isn't it fair? Now we finally have real equality between men and women!

It's true that actresses are paid less than actors, and it seems that this trend will continue. So now the movie industry has decided to reduce the work of actresses by 10%. In addition, female moviegoers will pay 10% less than male moviegoers. No actresses have complained about their pay since the policy began.

37

— What are you doing?
— Can't you see I'm looking in the mirror?
— Now I finally believe some statistics that I saw recently.
— What are you talking about?
— They show that men spend more time looking in the mirror than women do.
— I agree. But there's a big difference.
— What do you mean?
— Women look in the mirror to put on makeup, and men look in the mirror to reflect on who they are.

36

Korean people think education is the top priority. So it's natural that we send many students to the U.S.

China boasts the biggest population in the world. But the American people don't seem to know about it. We have to send many more students to prove it.

Our archrival, China, is sending a lot of students to the U.S. We have to send more students to catch up with them.

41

What's the difference between them? Women seem to know the difference between yes and no while men don't. So universities plan to strengthen grammar classes for MALE students.

42

What did I do wrong? I just got undressed because it was too hot! Then I wanted to see nude pictures of myself to see if my exercise program was having a good effect.

Let me go! I have a right to dress as I please and to take pictures of myself as I please!

I'm a smart phone. I'm so smart that everybody loves me. But when you abuse me by sending explicit pictures of yourself to others, it makes me very angry. You're going to pay a heavy price for your abuse!

50

— You went through a red light. I'm going to write you a ticket!
— The man behind me broke the same law. Why aren't you giving him a ticket?
— I'll get to him later.
— Why am I alone getting a ticket? Is it because I'm black?
— Well, you are more noticeable.
— This is not fair!
— Why don't you paint yourself white whenever you drive? It will help!

Way to go! Hey Buddy! Get out of the way! I'm in a hurry!

Think of these cartoons as scenes in a movie. The dialog has been scripted. Now we need actors to play the parts.

49

I don't want to be a referee in this dirty game! Neither of them is observing the rules

Everybody knows you lied about your emails. You are not qualified to be the President of the United States.

A liar is better than a womanizer! You're just a dirty grandpa! Drop out of the race immediately! You can always spend your time chasing skirts!

48

The purpose of this declaration of war on Earth is to provide a chance for Israel and Palestine to make a peace treaty. Just pretend to attack them!

— Oh my! The extraterrestrials are invading us!
— It's true! Let's band together to defeat them. We can live to fight each other another day.
— I agree. But don't forget we're archrivals! As soon as we prevail over them, we'll need to resume our war immediately!
— Ha, ha! We're on the same page!

158

43

Cheating is so rampant on the university campus that the Harvard faculty has decided that they'll no longer give exams and assignments in order to get rid of cheating. Instead, they will judge students' scholastic performance by how fast they surf the Internet because all knowledge is available online.

Solar-powered mouse: It boasts lightning speed, and no battery is needed. But if it's not sunny, it quickly becomes nonfunctional.

Nuclear-powered mouse: It goes thousands of years with no power failure, whether or not it's sunny.

I was an all-A student. But the university's new policy has made me drop out of school because I can't afford to buy a speedy mouse. I am a victim of today's nonsense!

44

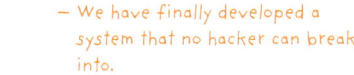

— We have finally developed a system that no hacker can break into.
— Don't you know I'm a computer genius? No system is safe from my hacking. My hacking skills will always outperform your security measures.
— I know it's a game of cat and mouse. May I make a suggestion?
— Yes, of course.
— Protecting our system costs a lot of money. We're willing to pay you regularly on the condition that you don't hack our system.
— Good idea! Then everybody wins!

S·y·n·o·p·s·i·s

These are the pictures you've seen in this chapter. It will be good speaking practice for you to talk about these pictures once again. Your teacher will ask you "What are they doing?" or "What does this picture mean?" or some other question. You can give a straight answer or you can use your imagination. The purpose is to allow free conversation; there is no "right" answer.

45

People have cut down all the trees in the world except for three trees.

I'm dying because of the lack of oxygen. Humans have destroyed every forest, and I am about to become extinct because of their brutality.

I don't have time to care about you! I have to cut down all the trees left and buy more oxygen ASAP. I'm running out of oxygen.

47

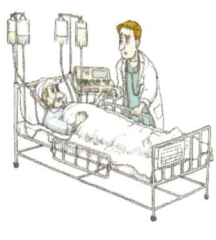

— I have severe pains all over!
— Don't worry. We'll take care of you.
— I want to be euthanized!
— No way! It's illegal here.
— Then how can I foot the bill? I'm broke!
— You're broke?
— Yes, absolutely!
— Then we have a way to save on your medical bills.
— What do you mean?
— From now on, we'll prescribe only aspirin, and then you'll pass away in a couple of days.

46

I agree. Something must be done for our survival!

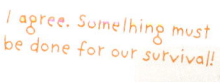

I'm worried about the bottom line and the increasing competition among the cartels!

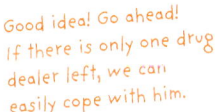

Good idea! Go ahead! If there is only one drug dealer left, we can easily cope with him.

Let's have a gunfight and let the winner monopolize the drug market! That's a fair solution, isn't it?

57

Artificial intelligence has now beaten humans at both chess and baduk, so I'm the last hope of mankind! I have to win in order to prove that human beings are still better than robots!

No way! Humans will have to kneel down before us creatures of artificial intelligence. We know all your weaknesses too well! You have created a MONSTER!

52

— As the President of the United States of America, I feel that we have a duty to pay reparations to the descendants of black slaves.
— Don't you think we've already paid them back?
— What do you mean?
— We've produced millions of black millionaires. Furthermore, we elected a black president for the first time in history! Isn't that enough?

60

— Why are you hesitating? Go ahead! Put me out of my misery!
— You'll have to wait. We need to get some more lethal chemicals.
— I'm scared stiff from all this waiting! Why don't you just hang me? It's quicker.
— No way! That's too cruel, and nobody wants to put the rope around your neck.
— Then use the electric chair!
— That's too inhumane, and besides, we don't have an uninterruptible power supply.
— Then put me before a firing squad!
— That's too brutal, and all the sharpshooters are on leave now.

Think of these cartoons as scenes in a movie. The dialog has been scripted. Now we need actors to play the parts.

59

This is the wall that I've made with the bricks of patriotism. It's strong and high enough to keep illegal immigrants out of our country. It will keep our country safe and secure!

Your patriotism is just a euphemism for hatred and prejudice. You've forgotten that your grandfather, mother, and wife were all immigrants to America! Get out of my way! I have to bulldoze this wall for the betterment of mankind.

58

Not yet! You aren't strong enough to knock me out of first place. Don't you see I have state-of-the-art products like iPhones and Boeing airplanes that you don't have?

Hey, Chinese! Don't try to accomplish a "MISSION IMPOSSIBLE." I tried to surpass America in the 70s and 80s, only to fail. Don't bite off more than you can chew!

Hey, American! Get off your pedestal! Now I'm the number one country in the world!

53

I'm not feeling well. I ache all over. You're harassing me with polluted air and water and cutting down all the trees. I can barely breathe. Do you call this sort of destruction "DEVELOPMENT"? How stupid are you? I can't survive unless you stop this kind of harrowing destruction immediately.

The Doomsday Clock is ticking! Let's leave and find a new colony in space.

Don't worry! Our planet is strong enough to hang on for another millennium! He's just pretending to be sick.

54

I'm sick and tired of parading down the street like this every day for tourists to gawk at. I want to resign!

No way! Then who will employ us? We'll be jobless!

Your Majesty! It is such a great honor to see you! Can I take a picture of you?

S·Y·N·O·P·S·I·S

These are the pictures you've seen in this chapter. It will be good speaking practice for you to talk about these pictures once again. Your teacher will ask you "What are they doing?" or "What does this picture mean?" or some other question. You can give a straight answer or you can use your imagination. The purpose is to allow free conversation; there is no "right" answer.

S·Y·N·O·P·S·I·S

55

Hurry up! Who are you talking to?

I'm so happy I'm almost there!

I can't hold on any longer! I wish I were at home!

— I'm the god of this mountain, and this is my residence! Stop disturbing my tranquility! Go down immediately!
— No way! I paid $25,000 for this climb! And I have to take a selfie on the summit.
— If you don't follow my advice, I will punish you!
— Punish me? What punishment could you give?
— An avalanche will bury you all!

57

If I play God saying, "I'm the messenger of God," people seem to believe it. They respect me and give me a lot of money. Scientology is the purest religion in the world! Don't you know Tom Cruise is a scientology enthusiast? And he is both famous and rich!

Ridiculous! I don't have to play God and shout "I'm the messenger of God." I just sit here, and people give me money. I know they regard me as a representative of God. Why else would they give me money?

People call me a pet dog. But I think I'm actually their god. They feed me when I'm hungry, bathe me when I'm dirty, treat me when I'm sick, and always love me unconditionally. What name can I call myself except god? Furthermore, if people treated me badly they would go to jail for animal cruelty!

56

Science and religion shake hands for the welfare of mankind. They are no longer rivals but friends. We promise to respect each other and understand each other. Remember the words of Einstein: "Science without religion is lame; religion without science is blind."

61

— You're under arrest.
— Why? I didn't do anything wrong!
— Don't you know that wearing a veil in public places is illegal?
— The man on the motorcycle is wearing a head covering too!
— That's a helmet, and it's required by law for safety.
— I wear the veil for the same purpose: SAFETY!
— What do you mean?
— If I wear it, Muhammad will protect me under any circumstances!

62

— What are you doing?
— I'm practicing driving with this video game!
— Don't you know women are not allowed to drive in our country?
— I know. But I'm preparing for my future! I'm sure the day will come when women can drive.
— Oh, don't start a trend. If word gets around, the government will prohibit this game.

70

I'm Gimbap from Korea. I have every necessary type of nutrition you need. I'm easy to make and carry, so I'm sure I'll replace every dish in the world the moment people learn about me.

I'm the Korean traditional food Kimchi! I'm healthy and harmonious with other foods. People around the world are crazy about me.

I come from Italy. I'm the essence of nutrition. But I'm wrongly accused of fattening people up.

I'm a traditional American food and taste delicious. But I'm a bit expensive, so not everybody can enjoy me.

I'm the most popular food in the world. I'm so nutritious that people don't have to worry about their health if they eat me alone. Furthermore, I'm cheap and fast! But I'm sad when people call me "junk food."

Think of these cartoons as scenes in a movie. The dialog has been scripted. Now we need actors to play the parts.

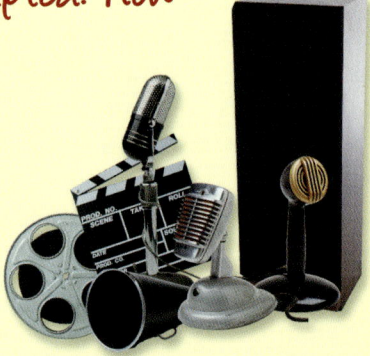

69

— They are immigrating to Mars!
— Good news! Once they have all moved to Mars, this place is ours. We can rebuild our planet, and we can live comfortably without them.
— They were so stupid to have polluted the earth! What a senseless waste!
— Men don't realize the importance of what they have until they lose it.

Don't be so sad! First we'll move to Mars, and later, if necessary, we can move to other planets. There are still billions of planets we can inhabit in space. We have destroyed just one planet!

68

When chemical warfare broke out, I didn't have to worry because I was rich enough and smart enough to buy the latest gas mask. I WAS RIGHT. Now everybody has died from toxic gases except me. What should I do now? I want to move to another planet, and I still have enough money to buy a space shuttle. But I have no friends anymore. I wish I had bought gas masks for them, but it's too late! There are just some things you can't do over.

63

- Today is the last day with you, Honey. Goodbye!
- What are you doing? Are you going to hang yourself? Don't do that!
- I feel helpless! Nobody loves me, understands me, or supports me…. There's no reason to live anymore.
- I feel helpless too! But I'll never take my life.
- Why not?
- I love myself so much that I can OVERCOME any difficulties!

64

I'm going to arrest you because you're illegal!

Ridiculous! We have the same talent for relieving people's suffering. And you're legal and I'm illegal? It's totally unfair!

I've been approved by the FDA, but you're too risky to be legalized.

Don't you know I'm more loved by people because I'm stronger than you and also easier to get? I'm available on every street corner in our country. The moment I'm legalized, you'll disappear in a moment.

S·Y·N·O·P·S·I·S

These are the pictures you've seen in this chapter. It will be good speaking practice for you to talk about these pictures once again. Your teacher will ask you "What are they doing?" or "What does this picture mean?" or some other question. You can give a straight answer or you can use your imagination. The purpose is to allow free conversation: there is no "right" answer.

65

Get out! This is our land because we were the first to plant our flag!

That's right. This is ours. First come, first served!

Just a moment! I'm almost there!

I'm going to fly my flag there. Why don't you move over a bit and make room for me!

It's so crowded there! I'm going to fly my flag here on an iceberg. Why don't you come over here! There are so many icebergs floating around unoccupied.

67

Don't be scared. Buddha is in your mind. Accept your destiny with tranquility.

Are you guys crazy? We're sinking! Stop praying and start bailing out water!

Even if you don't save us, I won't blame you, because I'll be able to see you in heaven!

I'm not afraid of any storm like this. I've prayed five times every day during my life, so I'm sure that Muhammad will save me at least, even if he can't save us all.

66

Stop! Don't you realize that your dispute has put the whole world in danger? We can settle any issue at the table by dialogue!

Get out, Mr. Obama! This is none of your business! We have no choice but to use our nuclear weapons to settle our territorial disagreements.

We're willing to use nuclear weapons too. Mr. Obama, can we borrow some nuclear bombs? We're afraid our rival has more bombs than we have.

LIS KOREA에서 나온
DISCUSSION TEXTBOOK

LIS KOREA는 토론 학습 교재 전문 출판사 입니다.

중고급 어린이 들을 위한 독창적인 영어교재

New Children's Talk(1), (2), (3)

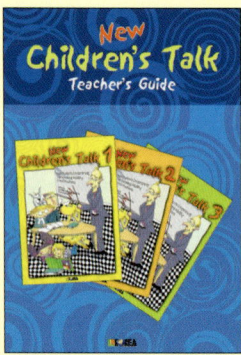

교사용

New Children's Talk(TG)

- 일상생활에서 벌어지는 상황들을 다양한 포멧에 맞추어서 많은 Speaking Chance를 제공합니다.
- 암기위주의 영어가 아니라 자기의견을 만들어 낼 수 있는 포멧들을 제공합니다.

청소년의 세계와 그들의 생각 관심사들을 토론으로

Chat Room for Teens (1)(2)(3)

- New Children's Talk를 배운 학생들이 Teen Talk를 쉽게 익힐 수 있는 선행학습교재로 사용할 수 있도록 구성
- 학습의 재미와 능률을 높이기 위해 다양한 그림들과 그것들을 바탕으로한 토론들 그리고 실제 많은 상황에서 발생하는 대화들과 수많은 지문들을 바탕으로 토론의 다양성을 확보

LIS KOREA에서 나온
DISCUSSION TEXTBOOK

LIS KOREA는 토론 학습 교재 전문 출판사 입니다.

 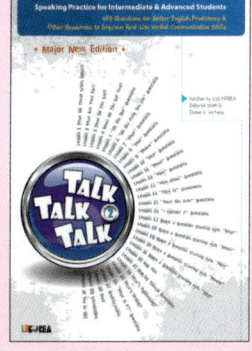

자유토론을 위한 훈련과정
Talk Talk Talk (1), (2)

- Express Yourself/Let's talk/What Do You Think?
  과정을 무리없이 이수하기 위한 예비단계로서 자유토론에 대비하기 위한 많은 훈련과정을 포함하고 있다.
- 여러상황에 맞는 다양한 질문을 학생들에게 던짐으로서 질문과 응답들의 패턴을 이해하고 습득케 하고자 했다.
- Express Yourself/Let's talk/What Do You Think?의 주요 훈련 목표 중 하나인 어떤 영어 단어나 문장을 토론자 스스로 다시 설명하는 훈련에 중점을 두었다.

Talk Talk Talk의 선생님 교재
Teacher's Guide for Talk Talk Talk 1&2

- 각권 25개의 이슈와 각 이슈에 대한 다양한 토론주제를 제공하였습니다.
- 토론 주제에 대한 다양한 Opinion Samples를 달아 학습자들에게 도움을 주고자 했습니다.
- 각각의 이슈마다 그와 연관된 Dialogue를 첨부하여 학습자들이 다양한 구어체의 표현을 익히도록 했습니다.

LIS KOREA 에서 나온
DISCUSSION TEXTBOOK

LIS KOREA 는 토론 학습 교재 전문 출판사 입니다.

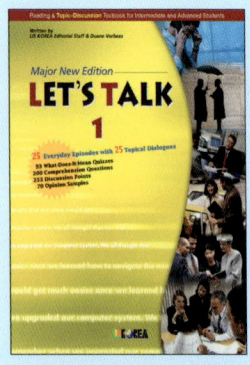 

중고급 토론교재의 결정판
LET'S TALK! (1), (2)

- 실생활과 아주 밀접하고 분명한 의견 대립이 나올수 있는 주제를 선정 고급 토론 영어를 위한 기초를 가질 수 있도록 구성.
- 토론 영어의 기초 단계인 영어로 설명하는 힘을 길러주기 위해 "What Does It Mean?"을 삽입.

■ Question에서는 제시된 주제에 대한 이해력 측정뿐만 아니라 한 주제에 대한 깊이있는 토론에 대비하는 힘을 길러 주고자 했다.
■ Discussion Points에서는 주어진 주제에 대한 토론 포인트는 물론이고 그와 연관된 많은 주제 제공
■ Opinion Samples에서는 학습자들이 주어진 주제에 대해 토론을 준비할 수 있도록 만은 찬반 의견과 참고 의견들을 제시하고 있다.
■ 어려운 표현이나 Idiomatic Expressions에 대해 각주에 충분한 영어 설명을 달아 학습자들로 하여금 이해가 쉽도록 하였다.

중급자들을 위한 토론교재
SPEAK YOUR MIND (1) (2)

■ 일상적이며 쉬운 주제들을 선정하여 간결하게 정리했음.
■ 대표 주제에 대한 질문과 대답을 여론조사 형식으로 꾸며 독자들이 쉽게 주제에 접근할 수 있도록 했음.
■ 모든 주제들에 찬반의견을 달아 독자들의 다양한 의견을 접할 수 있도록 했음.

LIS KOREA에서 나온
DISCUSSION TEXTBOOK

LIS KOREA는 토론 학습 교재 전문 출판사 입니다.

청소년을 위한 토론교재
New Teen Talk (1), (2)

- 청소년 토론교재의 최고 높은 단계의 교재로서 각권 15개의 이슈속에 500개 이상의 토론주제를 제시 합니다.
- 각 권에 포함된 9개의 포멧은 (What Does It Mean? / Comprehension/ Teen Talk / Opinion Samples / Dialog / Read& Discuss/ Pictures Talk / What's Your Advice? /Synopsis/) 각각의 특징에 맞는 다양하고 흥미로운 토론 주제를 제공합니다.

설명간결한 형식의 새로운 토론교재
Express Yourself Directly (1), (2)

- Pictures Talk 섹션에서는 큰 주제에 대한 warm-up 주제들을 선정하여 그림과 함께 제시하여 본주제에 쉽게 접근할 수 있도록 했습니다.
- Express Yourself Directly 섹션에서는 Pictures Talk 섹션에서 다루지 않은 좀더 깊은 주제를 선정하여 심도있는 토론이 되도록 했습니다.
- Let's Talk Funny 색션에서는 본 주제와 관련있는 재미있는 이야기를 실어 가벼운 토론과 함께 긴장을 풀도록 했습니다.

- What Does It Mean?에서는 본 주제와 관련된 Food For Thought를 제공하여 학습자들이 자유롭게 토론 할수 있도록 했으면 다양한 의견이 나올 수 있는 문구 들을 제시하였습니다.
- 마지막으로 Synopsis에서는 (전체 400의 그림으로 구성) 각 그림에 대한 설명을 영어로 명쾌하게 제시 하여 학습자로 하여금 주제에 대한 최종 복습을 할 수 있도록 했습니다.

LIS KOREA에서 나온
DISCUSSION TEXTBOOK

LIS KOREA는 토론 학습 교재 전문 출판사 입니다.

본격적인 비지니스 토론 교재
LET'S TALK BUSINESS

- 20개의 현대 비즈니스 주제가 78개의 Talking Points를 제공합니다.
- 수 백 개의 다양한 어휘와 표현들이 예문과 함께 어우러져 Self-study를 가능하게 합니다.
- 20개의 Topical Dialogue별도 수록

재미있는 창작 이야기로 토론의 즐거움을
LET'S TALK FUNNY

- 70개의 재미있는 창작 이야기가 수 백 개의 토론 이슈와 어우러져 독자들에게 재미있게 영어로 토론할 수 있는 기회를 제공합니다.
- 또한 우리생활에 감추어져 있던 또 다른 50개의 Thinking Points를 제공하여 발상을 전환할 수 있는 계기가 되도록 했습니다.

LIS KOREA에서 나온
DISCUSSION TEXTBOOK

LIS KOREA는 토론 학습 교재 전문 출판사 입니다.

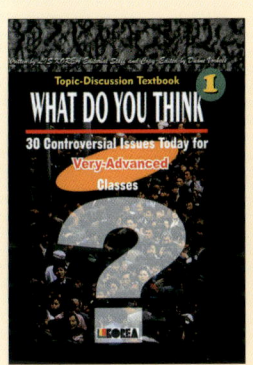 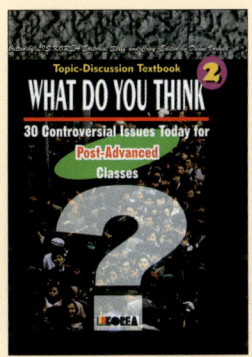

고급 토론 교재의 완결판
What Do You Think? (1), (2)

- Let's talk를 끝낸 학습자들이 좀더 시사적이며 깊이있는 문제들에 대해 토론할 수 있도록 구성
- 토론 영어의 기초단계인 영어로 설명하는 힘을 길러 주기 위해 What Does It Mean?을 삽입
- Question에서는 제시된 주제에 대한 이해력 측정 뿐만 아니라 한 주제에 대한 깊이있는 토론에 대비 하는 힘을 길러 주고자 했다.

- What Do You Think?에서는 주어진 주제에 대한 토론 포인트는 물론이고 그와 연관된 많은 주제 제공
- Opinion Samples에서는 학습자들이 주어진 주제에 대해 토론을 준비할 수 있도록 만은 찬반의견과 참고 의견들을 제시하고 있다.
- 어려운 표현이나 Idiomatic Expressions에 대해 각주에 충분한 영어 설명을 달아 학습지들로 하여금 이해가 쉽도록 하였다.

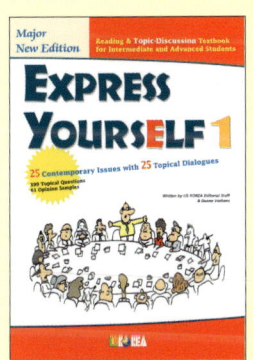 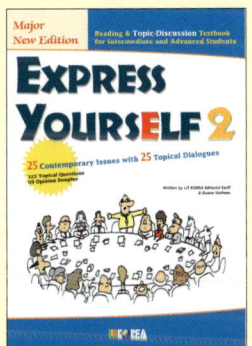

토론교재의 베스트셀러
EXPRESS YOURSELF (1), (2)

- 각권 25개의 이슈와 각 이슈에 대한 다양한 토론주제를 제공하였습니다.
- 토론 주제에 대한 다양한 Opinion Samples를 달아 학습자들에게 도움을 주고자 했습니다.
- 각각의 이슈마다 그와 연관된 Dialogue를 첨부하여 학습자들이 다양한 구어체의 표현을 익히도록 했습니다.

OPEN TO DEBATE 2

초판 1쇄 인쇄 : 2017년 6월 1일 인쇄
초판 1쇄 발행 : 2017년 6월 5일 발행
지 은 이 : Neal D. Williams
펴 낸 곳 : (도서출판) 리스코리아
펴 낸 이 : 조은예
등 록 : 남양주 제 399-2011-000003호
전 화 : (0502) 423-7947
일러스트레이터 : 김기환
편 집 디 자 인 : 이명금, 전정애
인 쇄 : (주)미광원색

www.liskorea.com

All rights reserved. No part of this book may be reproduced, stored in a retrieval system, or transmitted in any form or by any means, electronic, mechanical, photocopying, recording or otherwise, without the prior permission in writing of the Publisher.